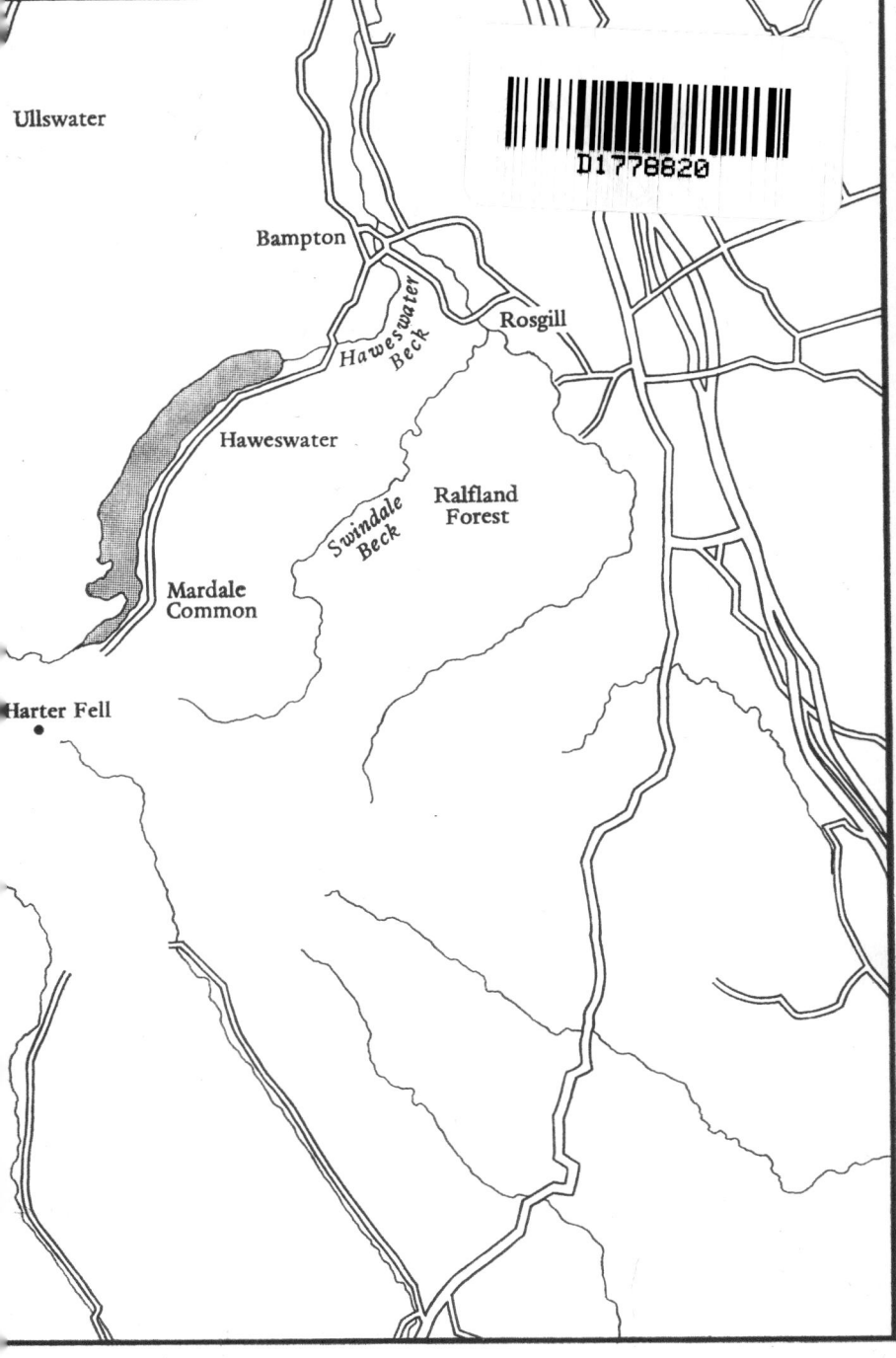

Hunter of Harter Fell

To Steve.
Xmas 1984

Love Mom &
   Dad

JOSEPH E. CHIPPERFIELD

Hunter of Harter Fell

Illustrated by Victor Ambrus

HUTCHINSON OF LONDON

Hutchinson & Co (Publishers) Ltd
3 Fitzroy Square, London W1

London Melbourne Sydney Auckland
Wellington Johannesburg and agencies
throughout the world

First published 1976
© Joseph E. Chipperfield 1976

Illustrations © Hutchinson & Co
(Publishers) Ltd, 1976

Set in Monotype Baskerville

Printed in Great Britain by
The Anchor Press Ltd and bound by
Wm Brendon & Son Ltd
both of Tiptree, Essex

ISBN 0 09 127680 2

For
Michael and Jane
in the fond hope that their dream
of
LANGHOLM
may yet come true somewhere
in
Dumfries-shire

ALSO BY JOSEPH E. CHIPPERFIELD

Storm of Dancerwood
Greatheart
Beyond the Timberland Trail
Greeka: Eagle of the Hebrides
Grey Chieftain
Windruff of Links Tor
Silver Star
Rooloo: Stag of the Dark Water
Dark Fury: Stallion of Lost River Valley
The Story of a Great Ship
Wolf of Badenoch
Ghost Horse: Stallion of the Oregon Trail
Grasson: Golden Eagle of the North
Seokoo of the Black Wind
Sabre of Storm Valley
Checoba: Stallion of the Comanche
Boru: Dog of the O'Malley
Lone Stands the Glen
Rex of Larkbarrow
Storm Island
Banner: The Pacing White Stallion
Lobo: Wolf of the Wind River Range

AUTHOR'S NOTE

Whilst actual place names have been used in this story which can be readily identified in the Lake District of England, the book is in actual fact a work of fiction, and all the characters are entirely fictitious. This applies especially to any character being given a special place in the community, and no reference to any person holding a similar office or following a similar occupation is intended, whether living or recently dead.

J.E.C.

CONTENTS

PART ONE
ALONE UPON THE CLOUDED HILLS
11

PART TWO
COMPANIONS IN THE HOUR OF NEED
63

PART THREE
RETURN TO THE LOCH AND RIVER
107

PART ONE

Alone Upon the Clouded Hills

I

In the hour before dawn, a noisy beck ran over pebbles and stones rounded by the passing years. In that hour, just before the new day crept over the dales, the voice of the turbulent stream roused from restless, troubled sleep the nervous dog who lay with his nose thrust into a bushy tail. He raised his head and shivered. It was chilly, and despite his thick coat, he was reluctant to leave the warm hollow he had made for himself.

Daylight began to make a dark silhouette of the long escarpment that raised itself to the peak of Helvellyn far over on the Cumbrian Range. Moment by moment, the fiery conflagration behind the mountains of the east grew in strength and splendour, glowing first with red, then gold. At last, with dazzling tongues of light, the flames unfurled on the horizon. Soon afterwards the sun was up. With it the world stirred in earnest, starting with the calling of a curlew whistling up loud and plaintive from the locality of the swampland about Low Harston, rousing the dozing alsatian to a confused alertness and panic that fed anew on his conscious memory pattern of the last few days.

There was little room in the narrow cave he had adopted as a temporary refuge since becoming lost in this utterly hostile hinterland of mountain and lake. Although the dog was unaware of it, the hostility sprang not so much from the different aspect of his surroundings, but from the long established routine he had followed with his master north of the border when, after a day out among mountains and lochs, they returned home at night to a large comfortable house. It was the master he missed most of all, then the security of the house. In this place, he had neither master nor home, and he yearned for both with something closely akin to despair. If only he could pick up some scent that was familiar and lead him back to the place where he had last seen his master! The fret in him drove him out of the cave to test once again the atmosphere.

He shivered once more as a chill wind struck him, and the fact was gradually sinking into his canine consciousness that in spite of his size and strength, he had been thoroughly spoiled by good living. Reared in a well-ordered household, and the devoted companion of an over-indulgent master, chosen by him when young from a kennel of similar animals he bred, he was quite unused to this life of survival into which he had been so abruptly thrust.

The dog shook himself vigorously, and whined, preparing himself for another day of searching for some familiar track that would end his loneliness.

As he stood, sniffing the varying wind currents, a picture, sharpened by its vivid impression, came to life. It was his last conscious, but all-abiding memory of his master sitting as he so often did with his back against a boulder sketching a long stretch of inland water with a hill rising beyond it. There was a clump of dark pines at the water's edge that bore a close resemblance to the Scots pines the dog had seen before in another place.

He lay on all fours, watching everything the man did, knowing that it was an occupation he enjoyed. It was quiet that morning save for a subdued murmur from the pines when the wind stirred them from off the hill. It might well have been the movement of one such trickle of wind, raising a strumming in the trees, that frightened a large mountain hare, squatting hidden nearby. Or perhaps it was the unexpected plop of a large fish far out in the lake. Whatever it was, the hare took fright. He was up and away, crossing the vision of the dog. In a second, the animal was on his feet and giving chase.

The pace was quick, although the hare was making a zigzag course towards the upper moorland. In scarcely a score of seconds, the lake was lost in the hollow that housed it, and the leaping hare, running for its life, led the excited dog up over the fells and along the winding valley of the Swindale Beck.

By that time, the heat of the hunt was on the dog before he discovered that he had travelled a great distance from the lake and the pines where his master was sketching. Still he continued to pursue that zigzagging hare, finally finding himself in the yawning expanse of Gatescarth Pass, with a thick mist coming up, blotting out each mountain outcrop and marked trail.

The dog came to a stumbling halt, the hare having vanished completely, swallowed up in the thickening mist. He stood very still, head held high as he tried to gain a bearing likely to lead him back to the lake and his master. All he could scent was damp earth and heather, and when he put his nose to the ground, the mist was already moving ahead of him, making it more difficult to pick up evidence of both his own and the hare's passage over it. The dampness was obliterating every recognizable scent that could assist him in finding his way back.

Even so, he did not give up. He continued to cast around, following the tracking instructions he had received from his master. He sniffed every stone, sought out every likely trail he could find, and did he but know it, was close to Gatescarth Pass when he was led away from it by the scent of another hare. The dog had sense enough to go back along it, thrilling with excitement as it grew cold. This he felt was the way he had come; but the hare had been disturbed by the agitated passing of the one that had been pursued by the dog, and had raced off towards the pass from the high fell now obscured by mist.

Thus, as the dog continued to follow what he still believed to be the trail of the hare he had originally hunted, he went farther and farther from the point he wished to reach, and after a long and fruitless search, came upon a mist-shrouded, craggy, pyramidal shape known as Harter Fell. He was tired, and his feet were sore from the rough ground he had traversed. As he paused by the outcrop, he thought he heard a voice, calling from a long way off. His ears went erect and his tail plumed. He thought it must be his master calling him. Then he knew he had been deceived by the call of a hill bird riding high above the mist.

He stood miserably uncertain of what to do next beneath the rocky outcrop. Then he dropped on all fours to rest, hearing the distant murmuring of a beck. So tired was he, and miserable, that he lowered his muzzle to his fore-paws, and giving a heavy sigh, closed his eyes.

When he awakened, the mist was trailing away from the moors and hills, and night was coming up behind a rising wind that rapidly swept clear the moorland of all low-lying vapour, leaving in the west large, white, woolly clouds.

Fortunately for the now very hungry dog, rabbits were feeding in numbers on a stretch of grassland not far from the fell and the beck.

The instincts of the born hunter drove away his despair. He crept forward slowly, ears erect and tail plumed, and was amongst them before they were conscious of his presence. The wind was in his favour, taking his scent in the opposite direction, and his velvet-footed movement enabled him to make a kill without effort.

Fortified by food which he ate on the spot, he drank from the beck and made his way back to the outcrop of rock. Feeling his way cautiously, he discovered a crevasse which, on further tentative examination, opened into a small cave. He dug feverishly amongst the rubble until he came to what appeared to be soft earth. There he made his bed, and turning round and round after the manner of his kind and those from whom, in the dim past, all dogs had sprung, he soon had a comfortable enough hollow in which to curl up and sleep. With a full stomach, he did not feel quite so unhappy, confident that in the morning light he would find the beloved master whom he had but temporarily lost.

That was all of three days ago, and now, as he stood outside the cave, his distress at still being lost was overwhelmed by the need to eat. He discerned rabbit footprints in the dewy heather, and as he put his nose down to examine them, found the scent warm and strong. He set off at once to hunt down his breakfast. He was not long in finding a large buck, nibbling the grass near the beck. The past three days had taught the dog much in the way of survival. All the old primitive instincts, long subdued by centuries of domesticity and being the helpmate of man, were rising in his subconscious and aiding him in a way that had never before been in his nature to pursue. With his body low to the ground, he crept forward silently, with the wind again in his favour, blowing directly in his face. Falling back on his hunkers, every muscle tense as he measured the distance between himself and his prey, his eyes narrowed as he concentrated on his next and final move. He pounced, his lithe body moving as if on springs. The rabbit never knew what struck him, nor did he know the identity of the creature whose jaws closed over his neck.

There had been no outcry from the stricken creature, and hardly a sound from the dog as he landed lightly on his feet. Still close to a normal domestic life, he ate quietly, merely tearing at the flesh. Soon the meaty parts of the rabbit had gone, and going to the beck to drink, he dipped his muzzle deeply into the running water as if to cleanse himself of any blood that might remain.

He was still the dog whose home was other than the wilderness.

Not many minutes later, he was casting around for some sign that might rouse in him some recollection of the scene likely to assist him on the way back to the lake where he had last been with his master. The vision of the man with his back set hard against the boulder, sketching, was clearly impressed on his memory. It meant so much to him; but the mist had done its work only too well. It had taken away the dog's sense of direction, and that other misleading scent he had mistakenly followed had worsened what had already become a precarious situation.

Even the distant sight of Gatescarth Pass, viewed from this higher angle, found no response in his memory pattern.

Once more, the dog was aware of every nerve in his body becoming tense with suspicion. He was alone in a place of which he knew nothing but the outcrop of rock where he slept, and the few tracks through the heather and the grassy spot by the beck. His past wanderings in search of that lake in the hollow had been taken in the wrong direction, and he had not ranged far enough, being frightened now of losing sight of Harter Fell, his only nightly refuge.

He was quite undecided on this particular morning of the direction he should take. The suspicion in him increased as he watched a stain of crimson light moving slowly over the weird formation of Kilnshaw Chimney beyond the ancient inn on the Kirkstone Pass road.

The dog was, in fact, frightened of the inn.

On the very first morning of being lost, he had almost walked into near disaster when he decided to approach it. As much as the building attracted him, it was the scent of wood-smoke that excited him the most, for it reminded him of the log-fire on the hearth back at his old home. His method of approach had been of extreme caution, for he was on strange territory. Crossing the beck at its shallowest point, he found himself among hollows that curved from west to east. For a while the inn had been hidden from sight, then on scrambling out of one of the hollows, he had a better view of the building.

Then he saw the road winding past it from Windermere to Ullswater, and knowing that his master daily used such roads, this became his objective more than the inn itself. Perhaps in his anguish of that first morning, his anxiety overruled his instincts of self-preservation. He loped more quickly, all previous caution forgotten; but the inn and the road were farther away than they seemed from the height at which he had viewed them.

He was in another deeper and narrower lateral valley before he was aware of the fact, heading straight for a small tent before which was a fire of reeking peat. Two youths of unkempt appearance were squatting around the fire. They jumped to their feet immediately they saw the dog, and being town-bred lads who had heard much of the Lakeland mountain rescue teams with their trained alsatians, they thought the dog one who had been put to round them up because the lighting of fires was practically an offence in the eyes of the wardens of the Lakeland National Forest Authority.

Having been brought up in a hard school and way of life, they had an inborn hatred of anything resembling authority, and picking up two formidable cudgels, they decided to take a chance and, if menaced, fight off the alsatian.

The dog, whilst startled at finding himself confronted by two aggressive young men, quickly took up a defensive stance. He had been well trained in obedience by his master, but never to be hostile. However, he had witnessed in the training ground at home more rigorous exercises for a few of the dogs his master had been selling at the time for work with the police.

He had been intrigued and wanted to join in, forgetting

that his role was that of a household pet, the companion of one man – his master! Yet, conscious of a well-loved hand restraining him, he had watched, and remembered so much that had taken place as preliminary tests. As a result his reactions were spontaneous the instant he sensed hostility in the attitude of the youths confronting him. In that brief fragment of time, he knew what he had to do. The hair on his shoulders stiffened, and his muzzle wrinkled in a silent snarl. There was no wavering in the look he gave the two. He was quietly sizing up the action they seemed intent on adopting, conscious of their fear of him.

'He's goin' to attack,' the more timid of the youths wailed as he fell back from his more violent companion.

'We'll soon settle him,' the other replied, not realizing he was now without support.

He moved forward menacingly, while his friend, dropping the cudgel he had been carrying, crouched behind the tent as if not wishing to see the impending conflict.

Acting almost against his will, he called out, 'Leave him alone, and perhaps he'll go away.'

Without taking his eyes off the dog, but knowing that he was now on his own, he shouted back the first answer that came to his lips, and decided to go it alone and play the hero. How he would boast when they got back to Liverpool. He, Micky Cotter, had beaten off single-handed a ferocious Lakeland police dog. That's how he would tell the tale.

Meanwhile, he noticed suspiciously that the dog had not moved any closer. Perhaps, like his pal cowering behind the tent, the animal was 'chickening out' in face of the heavy club he brandished. This idea gained a strong hold on his half-illiterate mind, giving him courage. He rushed forward vowing to give the alsatian a real, right battering. He'd show him!

Unfortunately for him, it all turned out the other way. The dog was remembering the relentless exercises those intended police dogs had undergone back home, remembering in great detail one very special method of attack demanded of them in circumstances similar to that which threatened him now.

The viciously inclined youth had not taken more than a dozen paces before the alsatian acted. He was perfectly balanced, his hind legs firmly set for the thrust he must make. There was no wrinkling of muzzle now to give warning of his intentions; only that steady look, unwavering and keenly sharpened to keep the attacker in focus. Just when the youth thought he had him, with the cudgel raised to crash down on his skull, the dog leapt. His fangs gripped the uplifted arm, gripped it above the wrist, the very impact throwing the lad back on his heels. The jaws closed and tightened, the dog swinging himself off his feet so that his entire weight – some one hundred and fifteen pounds – threw his opponent to the ground where he lay shivering and whimpering with fear now that the alsatian stood directly over him.

'Micky, ye're done for,' wailed his companion, making no attempt to go to his friend's assistance. He, like so many town-bred lads in their late teens, many in gangs and often in direct conflict with the police, was in dire fear of the dogs they used for mob control. This alsatian who had so expertly brought his pal, Micky Cotter, to the ground so quickly could be nothing other than a highly trained police dog.

Then, to the surprise of both, the dog withdrew, moving slowly up the fell down which he had come. He then stood looking down at the pair. The overthrown youth scrambled to his feet, holding the arm which the dog's fangs had bruised.

'Quick, Micky,' the other cried, emerging from behind the tent, unabashed at his display of cowardice, 'let's get out of here! He'll be barking soon . . . guiding the others.'

His friend, contemplating him surlily, merely uttered a crude reply, but nevertheless started to stamp out the fire, while the other took down the tent. The alsatian had not moved, but watched with interest these fumbling activities, and was still on the fell when, heavily laden with their equipment, the two took what they considered their best route to get away from the scene and climbed the opposite slope, making for the old coach road that led to Ambleside.

The dog also departed, spurred on by a growing apprehension of danger in the vicinity of the road and the inn.

He went back up the fell, travelling in an easterly direction, still hoping to pick up the trail he had taken when hunting the hare. By so doing, he lost his first real opportunity of ending his ordeal, for later that day a very harassed and clearly anxious man, in a car bearing a Scottish registration number, inquired at the inn if an alsatian had been seen in the vicinity. He explained the circumstances of how the animal had become lost, laying great emphasis on the fact that he wore a collar with his name and address engraved on it. 'He's quite friendly, so there is no need for anyone seeing him to be afraid of approaching him,' he concluded, rather sadly, the innkeeper thought.

The reply he got convinced him that the animal had gone off north and was undoubtedly lost in the undulating fells somewhere north-east of Ullswater.

He drove back to Patterdale more distressed than ever, resolving next day to get together a search party and thoroughly comb the dales leading up to Shap Summit.

2

All of three days, those events, so much in such a short space of time, but for the dog three days that were a lifetime of distress. In all his constant searching, his clambering up high fells in an effort to get a bearing, he had seen nothing resembling the lake and the pines where he had watched his master sketching.

As the fourth day grew brighter, he watched the changing of colour on Kilnshaw Chimney, noting in particular how it appeared to grow in stature. as the full light of day revealed its starkness against the background of sloping fells behind it.

Without being consciously aware of the fact, he had become older and wiser in the last three days. His sense of smell had become keener and his hearing more finely attuned to the many moorland sounds that held so many different meanings and life forms. Above all else, he was learning to put greater trust in the wind. It told him so many things. Just as important was the newly awakened awareness of the hunter in him.

He relished the flavour of moorland water in pools he came across, and the sharp coldness of the swiftly flowing becks that was somehow different from the burns across the border. He was quickly learning how to distinguish one place from another, not by vision alone, but by the shrill or gentle murmur of a beck, and soon was building up in his canine mind a pattern that was increased in familiarity by the feel of the ground beneath the pressure of his paws. Yet one marked antipathy remained. He still disliked having to kill his own food and got no satisfaction from eating a carcass that still retained the warmth of life in it, no matter how excited he had been at the beginning of the hunt.

That, were he able to understand it, was the major indignity he suffered from this unexpected life in the wild. In other ways, he was learning and even benefiting from it.

Vaguely, but inexorably, the past was slowly becoming interrelated to the present – not the past he had known in the happy companionship of a master and the security of a home – but a past going much farther back, a past that flowed in his bloodstream as it had in those who had been the very first dogs to submit to the domination of man.

All this might have taken a much stronger hold on him but for that closer past that had made of him one man's dog – a man he must at all costs find.

The morning wind was rising in chilly gusts, coming off Borrowdale. In a sudden surge of exhilaration, he turned and loped into it, but travelling well south of the place where helpers, enlisted by his master, were actively searching the moors from Loadpot Hill to Pooley Bridge on the eastern side of Ullswater.

It was rough country east of Gatescarth Pass towards Shap Fells. Reaching the head spring of Barrow Beck, the dog's pace slackened and when the wind veered he turned with it, finally rounding the head of Hawes Water and finding himself once again in the locality adjacent to Harter Fell. All he had achieved that morning was that he had covered a vaster stretch of country than on the three previous days, and was getting to know better the general terrain; but not once did he find or even approach near to the one lake he sought.

In rounding Hawes Water he did pass the southern extremity of what was known locally as High Street, the northern limits of which were, at that very moment, being carefully surveyed in the hope of finding him. He was tired, the edge of his earlier enthusiasm having been worn by the strenuous exercise he had taken over difficult ground. He paused, not noticing that the wind was no longer with him. His sides were heaving and his tongue a-loll, but his eyes roamed over nook and hollow until his gaze centred on a small enclosed valley that held in its midst, as if in a cup, a tarn, vividly blue. Along the grassy rim, a few sheep were peaceably grazing, while from high above came the plaintive mewing of a buzzard. Neither sheep nor buzzard held his attention. It was the valley and the tarn that attracted him most.

There was a tormenting intimacy about it, an intimacy so close and comforting that the alsatian could not refrain from uttering a hopeful whine as he moved slowly towards it.

For one passing moment a wisp of cloud passed over the face of the sun, and the lake lost its blueness and became momentarily dark. Then the dog knew. It was the lake alone that tormented him. He whimpered with disappointment, this time a disappointment so bitter that all power of functional movement ceased. He stood staring into empty space, seeing nothing, hearing nothing, knowing that he had again been deceived by what he, himself, had wanted to see. That stretch of water, no more than a tarn held in the grip of the hills with closely cropped grass surrounding it, only held that vague sense of intimacy in that it bore a slight similarity to the place he and his master often visited. It was an easy day's walk from their home at Langholm across the Scottish border.

'Roes Knowes', his master called the place, and it too had a small lake, just as vividly blue as this one and enclosed with grass just as green. It also was subjected to the same darkness when clouds crossed the sky, blotting out the sun.

Just one further memory pattern then, brief, but clearly visual in his canine consciousness . . . of himself sitting at his master's side while he painted the scene. After that, nothing! He only knew that the lake he saw now was not that at Roes Knowes, in spite of its gentle, isolated appearance. The pangs of bitter disappointment were such that his tail drooped until it lay between his hind legs like a flag stuck in surrender.

He turned miserably away, following a narrow beck that had its beginnings in another small tarn a little distance from the head of Hawes Water and within a couple of miles of Harter Fell.

The alsatian continued his leisurely climbing. He knew now that this had been another wasted day.

He was still lost amongst these voiceless hills!

Or was that an illusion too? Were the hills as voiceless as they appeared? As he climbed up towards Harter Fell, reaching yet another dale that dropped sharply to another – and this time a very small – mere a cry came wavering up to him. It sounded like an appeal for help, the despairing utterance of a creature in fear of death. The dog paused, the hair on his back bristling, surrounded by broken hillocks, and above, the fading sky and the ever-circling buzzard. The tarn was colourless, as if light never reached it; there were a few sedges at one place, the rest made up of a shingly shore-line. The broken stump of a long dead pine was like a solitary sentinel, keeping a never-ending watch over it. The Lakeland folk had a very special name for this place – a name so bad that it went far back in history. It was, moreover, seldom mentioned and the spot itself little visited.

The mere, for it could scarcely be termed a tarn, lay in a scoop of the valley, at one side guarded as it were by a craggy, lichen-green boulder on which was perched a ragged-winged raven, darting about, viciously snapping its beak at something it could not reach.

Again came the cry, whimpering at first, then rising into a gurgling howl, causing the raven to dance with savage intent and yet with impotent anger because he could not get at the thing that was crying out in dire distress.

The alsatian went racing down to the tarn, and with a honking scream of rage the raven went bustling out of the cleft in the fells, and vanished in agitated flight over the upper moorland. Forgotten now for one short instant was his deep grief for the master he had lost and had tried so hard to locate. At the same time he had become highly suspicious and not a trifle apprehensive, sensing something alien and wrong. The raven had not been hopping on the crown of the boulder without reason.

It was very silent now . . . Or was he mistaken? The boulder itself, lichen-covered and of irregular shape despite the hollowed summit that for endless centuries had held rain-water for the birds that dared to perch on it – and they were few – mainly ravens and hooded crows which the dog seemed to remember having heard his master call 'Corbies', loomed large in the alsatian's vision. It was a hideous disfigurement, whose summit hollow was now completely dry, but white with innumerable droppings. The deepest part of the tarn was at its foot, resembling a black hole in the water, the rest of the lake being of little depth.

As the alsatian approached the badly misshapen rock, he heard a sudden splashing and a despairing cry. He hastened around the outcrop and saw what had attracted the raven. A smallish dog was grappling desperately with both fore-feet to drag itself out of the deepened hollow, helped in one way by the very thing that should have taken it to the bottom. Around its scraggy neck, tied by a piece of rope, was a slab of Cumberland slate that had become securely lodged around the splintered base of the boulder.

The gipsy who had hoped to drown the creature had been much too nervous to see his work had been properly executed. He was terrified, being superstitious and in great fear of the place, and hurried away disturbed by the raven's honking call and the pitiful cries of the frightened dog. According to many of his tribe, the raven was the evil spirit of the tarn.

Gloom was gathering in the valley, adding to its grim appearance, and making the twisted boulder appear like the scarred face of some brooding demon. The surface of the tarn was growing darker and darker by the second, and the small dog was not only slowly choking to death, but was visibly losing its ability to hold on to the frail foothold it already had.

The alsatian acted with quickness. The gipsy had not only been inept in his task of tying the rope around the dog's neck, but had left a foot or two of slack between the animal and the slab of slate. At the first sound of the raven's call, he had panicked and thrown the dog a little short of the deepest point. In his extreme terror, the animal had rolled and was in that blackened hollow of the tarn, but held suspended when the flattish lump of heavy slate got firmly lodged under the base of the boulder. The alsatian trod cautiously towards the dog, meeting the piteous gaze from the already dimming eyes, and saw the loose end of rope between the animal's neck and the rock. He took it between his teeth and tugged. The pressure of partial strangulation was removed from the neck of the struggling animal, as the noose slackened. As the larger dog tugged, the other renewed with increased vigour his efforts to get a firmer grip on the shale. He was far too exhausted to do very much to help himself; but the alsatian's vastly superior strength gradually dragged him inch by inch from the watery hollow that was the source of the tarn.

Finally, after nearly five minutes of pulling and easing, the half-drowned dog had been hauled safely on to the bank. The alsatian did not leave it at that. He recognized at once a creature like himself, masterless and all but dead. He realized, however, that whilst the immediate pressure on the animal's throat had been eased, the rope still had the power to choke him should he recover sufficient strength to struggle free. At first the alsatian turned his attention to the slab of slate, but it was too securely wedged under the boulder to be dug out. Instinctively, the alsatian went back to the dog. He was still in a state of collapse and fatigue and lay with protuding tongue between clenched teeth, scarcely breathing.

Intuitively, the alsatian sniffed into the wet fur, his muzzle seeking for the rope. That also had been very clumsily tied, yet was sufficiently close to prevent the animal from pulling his head free, but certainly gave the alsatian enough space to get his lower jaw underneath it. He started to chew with determination, and carried on untiringly until the rope became frayed and eventually fell apart. During the entire proceedings the animal had not moved, but soon started to pant as air flowed unrestricted into his lungs.

For no better reason than it seemed the most natural thing to do, the alsatian started methodically to lick the wet fur as a bitch would cleanse the fur of the puppies she had brought into the world. Apart from taking much of the water from the outer covering of matted coat, the constant licking also brought warmth into the animal's thin body where before there had been a numbing chillness.

Ever since he was young himself, the alsatian had always shown a marked gentleness to the puppies brought up in his master's kennels, and this stricken creature, as far as the larger dog was concerned, was just another defenceless youngster wholly depending on help to survive. Just as the first star came out in the bowl of the sky, the animal responded to the treatment he was receiving, opened his eyes and raising his head a little saw as a silhouette the wolf-like shape beside him, licking him back to life.

For a second, he experienced once more a blind,

unreasoning awareness of panic; but the soft tongue went on with its gentle licking, soothing him until his fear was gone, and the blood began to glow more heatedly through his veins again.

He struggled to his feet, swaying from weakness and fear; but his huge companion was still beside him, licking his head now, and giving him a feeling of stability and comfort.

The young dog had, through the determination of the alsatian, gained a little confidence in himself, and shook his lean body, sending from it a shower of spray from what remained of the water. Although the larger dog could only see him as a dark shadow, the remembrance he had of him as he was pulled out of the water on to the shore was that of a cross-bred sheep-dog, barely nine months old.

In token of his gratitude, and almost by way of subservience, the young dog licked and sniffed the larger animal's muzzle, receiving a reassuring touch by way of returning the gesture. He was now much steadier on his feet, and when the alsatian moved away from the tarn and up towards the upper part of the valley that led to Harter Fell, the sheep-dog followed slowly, never falling too far behind. The alsatian was practically measuring his paces to allow the other to keep within distance, knowing that if that day had not been productive in tracing his master, it had, at least, given him a temporary companion.

That night, the sheep-dog slept beside the alsatian in the small cave on Harter Fell.

3

Outside the cave, an early morning drizzle was falling. Dampness invaded the small space under the fell, and instinctively the two dogs moved closer together. The alsatian, after his previous day's vigorous ranging over fell and dale, slept soundly; his companion was certainly more comfortable and more secure in feeling than he had been since he was stolen from a small farm dwelling above Rydal.

The gipsy who had taken him away from his home had been a cruel master, subject to violent outbursts of temper brought about by his wife's incessantly nagging tongue. It seemed the young dog was always the source of the trouble between them. Either he had taken something from the iron food pot that stood outside the makeshift tent in which they slept, and this he certainly did because they seldom thought of feeding him, or he failed to respond to the gipsy's complex instructions to make of him a satisfactory poaching animal. Neither man nor woman appeared to understand that he was little more than a puppy.

As a result, late one afternoon, after a terrific row during which blows had been exchanged, the gipsy in irate mood put a rope around the dog's neck and hauled him struggling up Rydal Fell, dragging him quickly across the road to Ullswater a little north of Kilnshaw Chimney and up the steeply rising fells between the southern end of High Street and Gatescarth Pass. His courage wavered when he finally came to the deep cleft with its grotesque rock and the silent mere. Since he had dragged the protesting dog so far without him getting his head free of the rope, he did little more than slip the noose a little nearer the throat, tying the other end to a slab of Cumbrian slate he found conveniently near.

In so doing, the noose was loosened a little, although the gipsy failed to notice it. Then with dramatic suddenness the raven appeared, eyes gleaming viciously and honking loudly, at the same time flying dangerously near. Suddenly the gipsy remembered all that was said of the place, and, grabbing hold of the defenceless dog, flung him yelping into what he thought was the deep pool at the foot of the rock.

He fled terror-stricken out of this narrow gut in the fells, hearing like an echo a despairing howl from the dog and the raven's continued calls. Little knowing the trail he followed and caring less, he did, however, arrive back at his temporary camping site to find a less ill-tempered wife awaiting him for supper. He sat cross-legged before the smoky fire, vowing in his heart to kill the raven next day, no matter the evil reputation of the valley and the tarn.

Much of this still lay like a recurring dream fantasy in the sleeping dog's mind, one scene following another with a confusing rapidity so that he whined and kicked until, half awake, he became conscious of the alsatian's body warmth beside him. He then vaguely remembered the animal's efforts to save him and entice him up the fell to this place of refuge under the massed rocks. Conscious of relief, he snuggled closer to the dog, and towards daybreak slept soundly while the drizzle went drifting away over the fells and lay in windless hollows as pockets of mist.

It still remained dark in the cave, and the dogs slept on.

As the new day grew in strength, there was no splendour in it. The sun when it came up was but a hazy glow

Alone Upon the Clouded Hills

behind a curtain of thinning cloud. The breeze, at ground level, was a constant flow of current over the fells, varying south-easterly to south. While the wind remained like this, the day would be fair, but if it changed into a westerly blow, bad weather could be expected. The early-morning drizzle had been just a warning.

The birds knew it; young leverets and elderly hares sat tight in their hollows, nervous and tense as curlews and lapwings started up an unceasing chorus. A greenshank, late in flight to the Scottish Highlands, passed over Harter Fell, uttering a sharp alarm note 'Tew . . . Tew . . . Tew . . .' as he witnessed a badger returning in stumbling haste to its sett in one of the dales.

For as long as five minutes the two dogs had been awake, listening to the constant calling of curlews and lapwings, but at the cry of the greenshank, they stretched themselves and ventured outside.

The damp morning air was filled with a hundred different scents, and the alsatian, knowing that he still had to search for his master, was a little impatient as he watched his companion testing the atmosphere. Now that his coat was dry, it was long and fluffy, ruffled a little as the breeze rounded the fell. Leggy as he was, his sheep-dog ancestry was clearly marked as he stood in much the same manner as the alsatian. In the right hands he would in all probability turn out to be a good working dog. The gipsy, with his cruelty, had not quite destroyed what was his birthright. Hunger, however, drove him to dig where the previous night the alsatian had unearthed the remains of a rabbit he had hidden away. As well he knew, nothing more remained, and further food would have to be hunted down.

There were clearly marked runways where animal feet had passed over the wet heather, and the alsatian uttered a low yelp that attracted the still digging sheep-dog who at once understood from the other's disinterested stance that nothing further remained in the cache that had only been an emergency food supply.

The alsatian then set off stealthily for the grassy patch beside the beck, the other dog adopting the same degree of movement as if sensing not danger, but the need for extreme quietness to achieve a set objective. In the space of a few seconds, he had learnt from the alsatian what the gipsy had been striving to instil into him by acts of harshness. The complete success of the manoeuvre became evident a moment later. To the surprise of both, they found a hare squatting near the edge of the beck, nibbling away at the choicest grass. It seemed that he alone was seeking food that morning.

A quiver of excitement rippled along the spine of the sheep-dog, and he wanted to yelp out and race at once to the kill: but the alsatian's alert attitude suppressed his impatience, making him understand that this was a hunting matter that required a very special method of attack. Already his companion was giving him sidelong glances of warning, for he had recognized at once that the creature by the beck was of the species that by running a devious course could so easily escape. Moreover, he had an intuitive feeling that it was the same hare that had led him away from his master, and thus the direct cause of his present discomfort and hunger.

Since that day he had learnt much through his misfortune, and had grown wise as to the ways of the wild. With another warning side glance at his companion, he sank low, his stomach almost touching the ground as he crawled towards the still unsuspecting hare. Behind him, the sheep-dog was doing likewise, silent, but still with excitement rippling along his spine. Like the alsatian, he also was learning fast. This was hunting by stealth and not by natural cunning and sheer fleetness of limb and foot.

Everything was in their favour. Even the wind – stronger now – was blowing sideways to them, carrying their scent well away from the hare. Crawling slowly and completely without sound over the wet bracken while avoiding the tufted heather, twenty yards became ten, and soon shortened to no more than five.

Suddenly the hare sat up with fore-paws held against its chest. An awareness of impending danger had come to him. His eyes were wide with fear – a fear that paralysed all bodily movement. He was unable to break free of that stupefying immobility and run.

The very same dog he had tempted to hunt him down a few days before was now to be his destroyer. Death came harshly to him with the alsatian's sudden leap, although he felt little pain.

The two dogs ate ravenously, and soon nothing but a few bones and wind-fingered fur remained. It would only be a matter of time before the grass would be as green and fresh as ever. Nature always renewed itself.

The two animals then lay quietly amongst the sparse bracken, staring drowsily, their bellies full and remembering little of the creature that had died so that they might live another day. After some ten minutes or so, the alsatian disclosed a sign of restlessness. He was once again being consumed by the desire to be on the move in search of his master. The sheep-dog also was more alert, the beck reminding him of his recent experience in the valley of the mere, and he was quite ready to go wherever the alsatian went.

Quite abruptly, the wind changed its direction, swinging from south-west to west, and the sensitive nostrils of the sheep-dog caught the scent of wood-smoke in the air. His companion was aware of it too, and watched the young dog suspiciously as he jumped to his feet, sniffing eagerly. The alsatian rose, knowing well enough the origin of the taint in the wind that added to his mistrust.

It was obvious to him that the sheep-dog wanted to investigate the source of the wood-smoke. It was at this stage that the alsatian remembered the road. Since he had failed to locate his master on the fells and in the dales, and knowing that he drove that car of his to many of the places they had visited together, he might find on the road what he would now like most to see – the car!

When the sheep-dog finally made a tentative move into the wind, the alsatian followed, keeping well to the rear. Whatever else the other animal might feel about the inn, for the alsatian it was still a potential place of danger.

The inn and the road were quite a distance from the region of Harter Fell, and it was some time before they reached the narrow valley where the alsatian had encountered the two campers.

Half an hour later, both dogs were within a hundred yards of the inn and the road that wound past it from Troutbeck Bridge to Ullswater. More suspicious than ever, the alsatian stood well hidden from the occupants of the inn. His odd fear of the place and Kilnshaw Chimney, a little distance away, made him extremely apprehensive. As a contrast, the sheep-dog showed signs of excitement. His head was held high as he tested the air currents with their smoky scent, and his tail waved to and fro. He had uncertain memory pictures of having been taken to it by his real owner who had thought him a 'very showy pup' and said so to the inmates over and over again. He had been made much of in that inn, and had lain near the blazing log-fire while his master meditatively supped his drink.

Looking at the alsatian as if inviting him to follow, he ran down from the ridge, halting within the actual confines of the grey-stoned wall.

The alsatian was not to be tempted; he just watched and waited. A man with a leather apron tied about him came out of the back door, and being on a higher level than the sheep-dog, saw him and called to somebody inside. A woman joined him, and shading her eyes against the light of the watery sun, shouted just one word 'Sheppy!' The call went echoing up the fells as if mocking the alsatian. At a second call, the sheep-dog leapt the low wall and went running up the narrow yard. He hesitated a moment, then with a body that wriggled and crawled but with a tail that wagged furiously, went up to the woman, who picked his thin frame up in her arms, and followed by the man, went into the kitchen.

The alsatian had no way of knowing that had he but followed the young dog, he would have been immediately recognized as the animal a man had been so anxiously enquiring about a few days before. As it was, he was unable to overcome his distrust, connecting the inn with the rocky upthrust of Kilnshaw Chimney. The impression it had made on him on that first morning of being alone on the fells was indelibly marked, and he could not shake off the influence it had on his canine consciousness, for it was virtually the very first thing he saw each morning since he had taken to sleeping in the cave under Harter Fell. With all his intelligence as a working dog, not only had he failed to find the one track he sought amidst this maze of fells and dales but, now in a more helpless condition, he was not prepared to go to a human habitation because of the threat he sensed existed in the vicinity of Kilnshaw Chimney.

Possibly future events would prove his instincts right; possibly not: but he was not prepared to take unjustified risks because a small sheep-dog had accepted the hospitality of the inn.

Standing hidden behind a hummocky ridge, the alsatian knew, with a heavy heart, that he was alone again. His companion for a single night had found somebody who knew him.

== 4 ==

When the alsatian finally decided to move down closer to the road, he did so by remaining in a deep valley that kept him well hidden from the inn. He felt no loneliness because he no longer had the sheep-dog as a companion. Their acquaintance had been much too brief for that, despite the dramatic nature of their meeting. Whilst each day took him farther and farther away from the hour when he became lost in this wilderness of fells and dales, they did not diminish in the slightest degree the memory he had of his master. Indeed, many of his characteristics were more sharply defined in his brain, and renewed his faith in the hope that one day they would meet again; but neither the despair and sense of desolation he at present experienced, nor the frantic desire to do something more in the way of action to bring that day nearer, made him lose his sense of caution. The closer he got to the road, the more nervously was he conscious that on the opposite hillside was the forbidding shape of Kilnshaw Chimney.

On reaching a break in the hummocky shoulder that hid both road and fell, he lay on all fours, concentrating his gaze on the highway, and strove to ignore the rocky landmark that caused him so much discomfort.

A couple of cars passed down towards Ullswater, but neither held his attention for they bore no resemblance to the very special vehicle he hoped to see. Yet the irony of this situation also lay in the fact that had he followed in their direction, he would have reached Patterdale where he and his master had been staying. The days spent seeking the trail back to the lake, and his ceaseless wandering over valley and fell, resulting only in his return to Harter Fell in the late evening, had impaired his sense of direction. So instead of following that road along its winding course northwards, he just lay watching the many cars that passed, knowing by the sound of each, more than by its shape and type, that it was not the conveyance his master used.

Patiently, the alsatian lay watching every movement along the road, still keeping himself well hidden. He scanned with deepening concentration a group of walkers, all carrying haversacks, trudging towards Ullswater. They were a happy, carefree crowd, all laughing and talking loudly.

When they had disappeared the dog felt lonelier than ever.

Gradually, there began to grow in him a restless desire to return to the hills, for it was on the fells he had lost his master, and as each car travelled down the road, not one resembling the vehicle he so longed to see, he began slowly to move back into the fells once again, hoping once more to find the dale and the tarn where his master had been sketching.

His tail hung limply, as if in his heart he was now despairing of ever finding the place. The one remaining expectation was that his master would find him, and if such were likely to happen, it would be on the fells or in the dales and not by the road. He was firmly convinced that the man would not give up trying. There was too strong a bond between them for that!

He continued on into the hinterland of hills doggedly.

It was at this same hour when another set off to vent his malicious spite on a raven. Unshaven and unkempt in appearance, he crept away from his gipsy tent, furtively looking from left to right as he tried in vain to conceal the shot-gun he carried. Fear struck into his heart every time he thought of his destination; but a grim, unrelenting determination to destroy the gipsy legend concerning the raven, drove him on. Like the camper, Micky Cotter, who, out of pure conceit, had challenged the alsatian to impress his companion and friends back home, the gipsy saw himself returning to his constantly nagging wife in the role of a hero. He, single-handed, had destroyed the raven who had become a legend amongst the travelling people, causing them to avoid the valley of the mere.

He walked with exaggerated caution, feeling the stock of the gun hard under his armpit. He was almost creeping when he skirted Kilnshaw Chimney, looking in all directions before he scuttled across the road. Soon afterwards he was hidden in a fold in the fells, but feeling more and more nervous as he came to the valley of the mere. Ahead of him, and not more than twenty minutes' walking distance away, was the alsatian.

The day had become brighter, the haze completely gone from both sun and sky. The earlier portent of possible rain had gone also.

At about the time the gipsy set out on his quest, two young people – a brother and sister on holiday from school – were following the Swindale Beck from their home at Rosgill. They were glad to be out for the day, the early morning being so doubtful that they thought they were likely to be confined to the house. This, for them, would have been a trying experience, being restricted in their activities. For the time being, while their parents were in the North of Scotland visiting an ailing relative, they were in the care of a very strict, house-proud aunt. As soon as the day brightened, they packed lunch packets, and now, with haversacks strapped to their backs, were determined to make the most of their day's outing. Their aunt had raised no objection, even standing in the porch, waving them off. This tiny gesture on her part had made them happy and carefree, and they chattered light-heartedly as they trudged along.

Being young and energetic, they were soon crossing Mardale Common, Hawes Water being hidden from view by the high ridge of hills that led to Gatescarth Pass. It was now becoming an upward climb, and Margaret suggested a rest. Jimmie, also a little breathless, but not anxious to admit to the fact, was only too happy to agree. They sat with their backs against a rock, the contours of the fells rising around them, and the yawning gap of the pass directly ahead.

Although they had no knowledge of it, the valley of the mere was less than a mile away over the westerly ridge; but once or twice they thought they could see a dark shape flying high over the spot.

Margaret said it was a buzzard; her brother retorted by saying it was more likely an old carrion crow.

His sister admitted he was right; they remained sitting with their backs against the rock, fascinated by the constant appearance of the bird so frequently rising above the distant line of fells.

'He's probably keeping watch over some late fledglings,' Jimmie said at last, reflectively, knowing nothing of the valley of the mere and the reputation it had.

'Should we go and look?' asked Margaret with excitement.

'Let's have a bite to eat first, then we'll go . . . at least to the top of the ridge. . . .'

They withdrew their wrapped lunches from their haversacks, and sat contentedly munching. In the half-hour or so they took, talking quietly about this and that, the bird made no further appearances, and their interest in him gradually waned.

In the meantime the alsatian was a mile or so south of Harter Fell, passing another small tarn and wading across the River Kent at a point where pebbles and gravel patches made a good causeway.

Way over beyond the rising ground that hid the valley

of the mere, a man sat hunched up and nervous, his gun resting across his knees.

Like the children, he had seen, from some distance away, the rising flight of the raven, and now that the bird was no longer visible, he imagined the creature squatting in the hollow of that rock beside the mere, awaiting his appearance. The superstitions that filled his mind took away the confidence he had in the gun. Supposing he missed! The creature would be on him like a wild demon, sweeping down and maybe clawing his eyes out and sending him mad and blind in a wild scramble across fells he could no longer see. So he sat in dread, staring across the one undulating ridge that hid the mere. Suddenly, as he watched aimlessly, the whole landscape ahead became aglow. Fold after fold rose about Harter Fell and Gatescarth Pass, everything that moved becoming almost outsize in appearance like the curlew that rose from somewhere near the mere, frightening the gipsy until the sunlight lit up its streaked and patterned plumage and he heard its lonely yet musical cry.

One thought was in the man's mind then. The raven had driven it off, and soon perhaps would appear from behind him and swoop down before he could bring his gun to his shoulder. Something else became visible in that sharp, spotlight glare – something like a wolf standing motionless on the high fell above the pass. The gipsy, his mind far removed from dogs at that moment, decided that the figure outlined against the sky might be a stray roe deer, or, more likely, one driven from the small herd he knew existed somewhere about Bowness.

He had heard of it happening often enough in other parts of the lakes where woodland was sufficiently dense to support and give them refuge, but never here! The distant figure remained so still that the gipsy's curiosity got the better of him, and a haunch of venison was better than a dead raven. Anyway, he could, as a salve to his conscience, still view the valley of the mere on his return, and, maybe approaching from a different quarter, get in a surprise shot at the bird. He refused to admit, even to himself, that he was relieved at the diversion caused by the intrusion of the animal on the fell, although he knew well enough that he had lost his enthusiasm to go right into the valley of the mere.

The direction the gipsy now took was a more southerly one, bringing him close to Harter Fell. His walking was different; he trod with greater care, using what little cover there was to keep himself hidden. He knew he would have to cross the head of the Swindale Beck if his assessment of the animal's position was correct. No mean poacher at any time of his wandering existence, he easily dropped into the quiet manner of a stalker intent on bringing down his prey, but was still wondering what exactly it was that stood so motionless. Already his imagination was ahead of him. He saw himself, with a limp roe deer slung over his shoulder, going up to the gipsy tent with a jaunty air. Let the devil himself take the raven! As he had told himself previously, a haunch of venison was even better than the doubtful pleasure he might get at killing a scraggy bird. Not that he really thought he would. It could well be the other way round, with a creature as vicious and tenacious as that raven of the mere.

In his detour, he discovered the falling ground from Harter Fell difficult to negotiate, and more often than not he found himself sliding with a gathering momentum that seemed to him dangerous in the extreme. He finally came to the southerly run of water that, east of the pass, joined up with the source stream that became the Swindale Beck.

By now he was in a foul mood. The gun was an encumbrance that jolted hard under the armpit every time he missed his footing. The water was flowing rapidly and deeper than he had supposed. Unlike the alsatian who when fording the River Kent had taken his time and used a causeway, the gipsy impatiently plunged through the water which reached over the tops of his boots, already well worn, and made his feet wetter than ever.

More than that, he had realized that he was on a part of the fells that was strange to him. Pausing in an effort to take his bearings, he looked for the high ridge that he imagined overlooked the pass. There was nothing visible on it, but he could just glimpse the outline of a higher fell beyond.

He moved forward with mingled fear and caution. . . . The gun was now held in one hand, ready for immediate use. The hill he was now so laboriously climbing was thick with heather, the stalks pricking his knees and legs.

He was panting heavily, and finally lay exhausted just below the summit of the ridge, knowing that a much higher escarpment lay on the other side. He could hear the distant murmuring of another beck – the westerly arm of the Swindale Beck that had its beginnings in the Gatescarth Pass itself.

'I'll rest up a wee bit before lookin',' he said on a husky intake of breath, experiencing once more a spasm of alarm. Apart from the wetness of his feet and legs, he was now aware of his shirt clinging damply to his back.

He shivered, gripping the gun more tenaciously than ever.

'I dunno what's come over me,' he muttered. 'I've pushed messel' too hard.'

He had unknowingly followed the swing of the fell and from the moment he crossed the first arm of the beck was on territory quite unknown to him. He did not realize that he was so close to the pass; nor did he know that just over the opposing ridge the ground fell away to the valley of the mere. Time too appeared to have lost all meaning.

He had no idea how long he had been in skirting Harter Fell after sighting the strange animal.

Rising himself on to one elbow, he peered fearfully over the summit, and dropped back out of sight quickly, his heart thumping spasmodically. He was amazed and very much frightened. The animal was still on the ridge, no longer motionless, but moving slowly towards Harter Fell. He seemed enormous to the gipsy, especially from the angle from which he viewed him. Moreover, because he had his nose testing out the ground, his shape was distorted, and not by any stretch of imagination could the gipsy identify his species. All he could see was a long sloping back and a bushy tail. The gipsy's perspective was all wrong; his line of vision distorted by hummocky ground. Of one thing he was certain. The creature was not a hill fox. He was much too huge.

He was forced to fall back on his original idea. It could be only a young deer; but its gait was curious. He could not remember ever having seen a roe deer walk in such a fashion. Maybe it was lame or something. Anyway, the animal was within range of gun-shot.

Using great care, he eased himself on to the top of the ridge. The dog was moving farther away, only his hind quarters being fully exposed. 'I'll lose him if I'm not careful,' the gipsy kept repeating. Trembling, but urged on by the insane desire to slay, he brought the gun to his shoulder and squeezed the trigger.

The man could not quite grasp what happened after that. He only knew he had scored a hit, for he saw the animal leap up, give a loud yelp, then limp over the skyline, going down into a dale a little distance from the valley of the mere. The gipsy was aware only of running down one incline and scrambling breathlessly up another. The animal he had hit had totally disappeared. Finally, he reached, in exhaustion, and drenched in perspiration, a high flat section of fell from which he could see, at least

a mile away, the road to Ullswater, with a beck running between him and it. Slightly north-west of the road was the unmistakable shape of Kilnshaw Chimney rising starkly on its knob of rising ground like a gnarled finger.

He sighed with relief. At last he new where he was on the fells.

Then he was conscious of a most curious effect from the shot. Echoes were coming back to him from ridge and high fell, some startlingly loud, some just quivering vibrations of sound. Panicking again, he took to running quickly, stumbling more often than not along a not too clearly defined heathery track striking due west.

By now he was badly scared, but could not understand why. Perhaps it was all because of the recurring shots. 'It must have bin a cussed lurcher I fired at!' he cried aloud. 'Couldn't have bin a deer . . . A lurcher. . . .' The words stuck in his throat, for he thought of coming face to face with a pain-maddened dog. It was then danger really did assail him, and not from a dog. Honking angrily at being disturbed, the raven from the mere flew above him, making a low swoop.

The gipsy shrieked out; the fells spun and the sunlight darkened. But his ears were still open to sound, the hoarse croaking of the outraged bird striking seemingly into his brain. He beat the air with the butt of his gun, the bird flying round and round, its ragged wings only an inch or two above his head. Then, as the raven flew off, one loosened feather falling on the gipsy, he stumbled to his knees and completely blacked out. . . .

5

Jimmie and Margaret Thornton were abruptly roused from their lazy drowsing by a sharp crack from a gun. Both sat up startled, Margaret clutching her brother's arm in fear. The shot had appeared to come from the direction of Shap Fells. Margaret said so, but her brother disagreed. 'It was nearer than that,' he said. Then as if to confuse them both, the fells flung back the echoes, each bounding and rebounding from north, south, east and west. From all this repeated din, one couldn't tell where the shot actually came from. Jimmie said so with a feeling of disappointment. He liked to be exact on details, and anything so disturbing as this caused him to distrust the evidence of his own ears. The echoes went on for a long time, and both saw the shape of the huge bird across the fell rise in agitated flight.

'I thought I heard a yelp after the shot,' Margaret said distressingly.

Her brother was inclined to agree. 'We'd better set off for Harter Fell and investigate,' he said hesitantly. 'We can look out over Shap Fells from the summit.'

They hastily repacked their haversacks, and were soon stumbling up the rough track leading to the fell. As they struggled on, pushing themselves a little harder than they should, there was no sign of life whatever ahead. They were sturdy outdoor children, the girl thirteen and her brother coming up to fifteen. They had always lived at Rosgill and were used to rough walking on the fells.

'It could have been a poacher,' Jimmie panted.

'Yes . . . but that yelp! It sounded like a wounded dog to me.'

'It certainly did, and we must make sure. You just can't leave an injured animal to die out here . . . perhaps in great pain.' He secretly cursed all poachers and gipsy campers who were the greatest offenders, getting whatever they could for the pot.

Something of what he was thinking was communicated to Margaret and both were instinctively spurred to greater effort until suddenly the girl stopped with a cry of dismay. She pointed to a slab of rock on which a bright-red spot of blood was visible.

'No matter how long it takes, we've got to find that animal,' Jimmie remarked grimly, his face expressing his seething indignation. 'He's probably gone up to Harter Fell for cover.'

Not far from the rock was a patch of soft, almost boggy ground on which the large pawmarks of a dog were firmly imprinted. Jimmie bent to examine them, exclaiming at once: 'They're a dog's all right. . . . A big dog at that.'

He then saw more imprints and spots of blood, all leading up to the high fell above them.

'Come on!' he said quickly. 'He's not so badly hurt he can't move. He *must* have made for the fell.'

The rise was steeper now, the whole area a series of deep valleys and sudden upward surges of rough climbing. The track was but a thread through the heather, but both noticed in those valleys where the ground was damp that the dog's footmarks were more deeply scored, as if he moved with increasing difficulty. Moreover, there were more blood spots, and it was on one such occasion, where the ground was boggy, they discovered the animal's hind foot appeared to drag a trifle, leaving behind blurred nail and toe impressions.

'He must be badly hurt!' Margaret cried out in distress.

'Not so badly hurt that he can't make with determination for the rock coverage on the fell. I'm sure that's where we'll find him,' Jimmie answered triumphantly.

'There are what you might call "caves" on Harter.'

By now droplets of blood were more in evidence, all seeming to lead in one direction. The two, excited at the prospect of finding the injured animal, and the girl comforted and reassured by her brother's confident manner and assumption, certainly felt more hopeful of success at the end of their journey, but was still, at the back of her mind, exceedingly anxious. She hoped with all her heart that the animal was indeed in hiding on Harter Fell.

Both were breathless when the summit was reached, and they were forced to cast about a little until another bloodstain was seen near a cleft in the rock. They dropped to their knees, Jimmie whispering, 'It's as I thought. He's hiding . . . possibly very frightened.' They peered into the darkness, the boy warning his sister to be very careful. 'If he's in pain, he might be vicious,' he said.

'We'll soon find out,' came the rather tense reply. Then she added: 'Have you the torch?'

Jimmie swung his rucksack around, rummaged in it for a second or two and then pulled out a bright, shining cylinder with a large magnifying lens. 'It's got a new battery in it too. I wouldn't want to get lost up here in the late evening without it and it could so easily happen if a sudden mist came down.'

Margaret asked him to shine it into the crevasse.

Jimmie did so cautiously, first of all keeping the light directed on the ground, then crawling to the entrance of the cleft, let the beam wander around slowly, while uttering soothing sounds calculated to allay the fears of any animal that might be hidden in there. As far as he was concerned, there could be no doubt now, for he could see drops of blood on the scree and heard a low whine that ended in a warning growl.

Pulling his handkerchief from his pocket, he gave it to Margaret, whispering: 'Go and soak it in the beck.

There's one quite near. I can hear it. You'd better do yours as well....'

She went quietly away to do his bidding, leaving him now directing the light from the torch on the wounded dog, who sensed he meant him no harm; and indeed, having always cherished a liking for children, listened to his voice while he went on methodically licking the injured flank.

'We'll soon have it well,' Jimmie was saying, remembering that his father had told him that a dog responded more to the tone level of the voice itself than to the actual words.

Margaret returned very silently indeed, her feet making no sound. Kneeling beside Jimmie, she asked: 'Is he there?' Her brother nodded. 'It's an alsatian,' he whispered. 'Possibly one of those alsatians they use on the fells to find climbers who get lost. Come up close and see for yourself.'

She did as he asked and peered into the gloom of the cave. The dog, aware of another presence, looked up, panting. His ears were erect, and his eyes glowed in the torchlight. Whatever else she might have expected to see, she saw not a frightened dog, nor one who cringed away, but returned look for look with complete trust. She began to think that he was expressing utter relief at having somebody with him. As if to enforce this feeling on her part, but mainly moved by the desire for contact and possibly a little comfort with human beings, he crawled forward a little to meet them, whimpering with pain as he did so.

'I think he wants us to help him,' Jimmie muttered with a note of sympathy in his voice. 'He's not too badly hurt, as I suspected. There are a few widespread pellets in the flank. He must have been too far away to get the full force of the shot. If only we had something to probe them out gently we might help him to get rid of them....'

Margaret pulled a clip from her hair, causing one lock

to fall over her eyes. Cleaning it briskly with her wet handkerchief, she asked her brother if it would be of any use.

Jimmie appeared doubtful for a moment, thinking mainly of the dog's reaction to having further pain inflicted on him. Better Margaret's suggestion, perhaps, than risk the pellets working themselves deeper into the flesh. 'It might work,' he replied, 'but you'll have to do it while I hold him. He might try and bite.'

Margaret shook her head confidently. 'He wouldn't. I'm sure of that.' Then, as if taking over complete control of the operation, she added: 'Fix the torch in the rock so that the light falls in the right place, and I'll try and get out the pellets as gently as I can. You pet him and talk to him while I do it. I'm quite sure he'll be all right.'

Still feeling uncertain as to the outcome, her brother did as she asked.

At the first probe, the dog growled, but made no attempt to struggle against the girl's efforts, nor did he try to thrust her hand away with his muzzle as Jimmie had expected. Vaguely, the animal realized she was trying to ease his discomfort, and the boy's hands moving rhythmically over his back, and his voice speaking to him soothingly, added to his trust in them. One by one the pellets were removed, but the bleeding had started up again. 'We'll soon stop that with our handkerchiefs as a sort of compress,' he said with assurance. Then, as if greatly surprised and with a complete change in his voice, he concluded; 'Gosh! He's been great. It must have hurt a bit doing that....'

Margaret was already sponging the wounded spots, and gradually the bleeding was becoming less; but the fur around the wounds was very sticky and matted.

'Keep on petting him,' she whispered to her brother. 'Let me have your flask, and I'll take it with mine to the beck, for he's surely in need of a drink after that ordeal.'

'Wash out the handkerchiefs as well,' he answered, giving her the flask.

'Of course, silly,' she replied at once. 'I've a feeling you think me lacking in brains.'

Jimmie grinned at her as she edged her way past him into the light. 'One thing I must admit,' he said. 'You're not lacking in courage. There's no girl I know who'd do what you did to a strange and wounded dog . . . an alsatian at that.'

'Silly again,' she retorted as she hastened to the beck. 'Anybody can see he's as gentle as could be, and intelligent enough to understand we were helping him.'

Jimmie was still running his hand over the dog's back. 'He's a very nice dog,' he said as Margaret crept in beside him. She nodded as she poured some water into the cup of the flask. The dog began to lap eagerly, and drank three such measures. The children then remembered the remainder of the sandwiches in their haversacks. These were quickly devoured by the animal, who was then given more water.

'Stay with him and keep making a fuss of him,' Jimmie said, 'while I go and gather some fern or heather to make his bed more comfortable. It can't be very comfortable in that hollow he's made for himself. We'll come back in the morning and see how he's getting on.'

'He might be away by then,' Margaret objected.

'Not he,' replied her brother firmly. 'That flank will be stiff for a day or two yet. He'll just have to rest up for a while, and it's my belief that with a comfortable bed instead of scree, he'll want to do nothing but just that.'

Whilst he was away, Margaret, wetting one of the handkerchiefs with water from the flask she had not used, started to cleanse as gently as she could the matted fur. The dog turned his head to watch her. Suddenly she felt his warm tongue licking her fingers, and knew that whatever happened in the future he would never forget her kindness to him. 'You're a lovely dog,' she whispered. 'I wonder how you came to get lost up here?'

He looked into her face and whined softly as if he understood what she was saying to him.

Impulsively, she hugged the dog against her, murmuring: 'I understand what you're trying to say. We'll be back tomorrow, and perhaps might have learnt something about you,' she ended in a whisper.

For a few moments longer, they both sat in silence, waiting for Jimmie to return, the girl's arms about the dog, his head resting on her shoulder.

Not long afterwards her brother had spread some moss and heather in the hollow where the dog had been lying since he became lost.

Before they left, they heard him licking the wounded flank, and both knew that he, himself, would get on with the healing process. Patting him gently and saying they would be seeing him next day, Jimmie and Margaret withdrew from the cleft on Harter Fell, to find the sun low in the west and twilight already marshalled in the hollows of the east.

'We must hurry,' Margaret said.

They quickened their steps once they reached the pass, and came out on to Mardale Common thinking of the dog.

6

Jimmie and Margaret were glad, on rounding the head of Hawes Water, to see the distant glimmer of lamp shine from Rosgill. The lights were few and far between, and the houses little more than straggling outposts from Bampton. Still, one of those houses was 'home' and as they were now conscious of the chill of evening, they would be glad of the log fire they were sure would be blazing in the hearth of the sitting room. A bleak, unuttered dismay at meeting with their aunt's displeasure at being so long away was less important than their concern for the injured dog who lay in the cave of Harter Fell.

They turned in at the gate leading to the grey-stoned house of reasonable proportions, and saw in the sitting room, the flickering blaze of the log fire that had been at the back of their minds.

As the remainder of the front part of the house was in darkness, Margaret murmured, 'Aunt Ellen must be in the kitchen. I wonder will she be angry?'

'You can bet on that,' Jimmie answered with a display of spirit. 'She's never really happy unless she has something to grumble about. Anyway, we got lost between Tebay and Shap where we had gone to watch the trains climbing the bank. We waited too long for a Scottish express that was running late, and in hurrying back, took the wrong track.'

His sister giggled.

'Do you ever tell the truth?' she asked.

'Indeed I do . . . mostly always,' her brother answered with some heat. 'It's only a small white lie I'm going to tell. We couldn't explain about the dog, could we?'

'I suppose not; but when did you exactly think up that tale?'

'The moment I came through the gate. I knew you wouldn't let me down.'

There was a short pause before Margaret finally replied. 'Now I feel as bad as you.'

'I can always rely on you,' Jimmie whispered, coming up to the kitchen door where lamplight gleamed, and their Aunt Ellen was bent over the stove. They saw the white cloth spread over the table, and places set for their evening meal. 'Gosh! I'm starving,' Jimmie said. They glanced at each other, both feeling the pangs of hunger.

To his astonishment, Jimmie's explanation was accepted with just one remark. 'I should have thought you've both been to Shap and Tebay often enough to make your way back home blindfolded.'

After washing themselves, a few seconds later they were sitting down to a hot and appetizing supper, and none of them had further time for speaking, their aunt disposing of a bowl of soup quickly, left them to go into the sitting room to ensure the fire was burning brightly.

Then their aunt came bustling back into the kitchen. 'Come on, you two!' she exclaimed. 'Finish up your suppers and go into the other room. There's a great fire going and it's a chilly sort of evening. I want to clear away.'

In no time they had finished their meal and were at the sink, Margaret washing up and Jimmie drying. Their aunt watched them, wondering at the sudden burst of activity, but glad of the help. 'Their parents will be home soon, I expect,' she said quietly to herself. 'Anyway, they're very good children considering how their father lets them do just what they like. . . .'

The children's Aunt Ellen apparently had no regrets for being a spinster, the only one of a family of three girls and one boy who was away in Canada. She was, to say the least, an excellent schoolmistress and one highly regarded by the education authorities.

Her mind was so occupied that she scarcely heard the children leave the kitchen, slipper-footed and walking unobtrusively.

Firelight flickered over the raftered ceiling of the sitting room, and before switching on the light, brother and sister moved over to the night-darkened windows and stared up to the Gatescarth Pass and Harter Fell that was high in the fold of the dales above it. At first they saw only the reflection of the firelight in the windows, then their own faces.

Their eyes now having become accustomed to the gloom outside, enabled them to glimpse vaguely the heavily darkened dales and rising out of them the fells like heavy shadows etched on canvas. Their thoughts were of the dog, who, did they but know it, still lay where they had left him, methodically licking his flank, but no longer feeling the pain while still remembering their gentleness and even the sound of their individual voices.

Yet behind all the events of that day, the killing of the hare, the loss of the collie to the inn, his injuries and the children finding and helping him, there was still, deep inside him, the ache and longing for his master . . . the master he must find! Even so, a little of the longing was assuaged by the instinctive knowledge that on the morrow the children would again be visiting him, and they might be able to help in the quest to find the valley and lake where his master had been sketching.

An hour later, he was asleep on the bed Jimmie had made comfortable for him, tired and utterly exhausted after a very, very strenuous day.

During the time Jimmie had been standing beside his sister at the window staring out across the indistinguishable fells and dales, a plan had been formulating in the boy's mind. He had known that it would have been completely useless just taking extra sandwiches to feed a dog so large as an alsatian. He'll want meat to keep up his strength, he thought; and the idea had no sooner entered into his mind than he thought of the store pantry – an outside abutment to the kitchen at the side of the house. The pantry in the kitchen itself always held most of the food required for the week, but that outside store pantry ...

He was thinking it should be well stocked, for just before his parents left for the north they had driven into Penrith and brought back a huge quantity of food, including half a carcass of lamb. Besides that half-carcass, there were tins of various foodstuffs and biscuits. Since this store pantry was well ventilated and protected from the sun, even on the warmest day both he and Margaret regarded it as an 'ice box'.

Aunt Ellen had not visited it yet, and part of that carcass would not be missed, nor perhaps, some of the tins of corned beef which could be taken with impunity. It was stealing, he knew, but that dog had to be fed.

Jimmie spoke in whispers of his plan to Margaret. She was at first horrified at the idea, then saw it as the only way out of their predicament.

'Supposing Aunt Ellen has already been in the store pantry and knows what's in there?' Margaret queried as this thought struck her.

'I'm pretty certain she hasn't. There's been no reason,' Jimmie replied. 'As you know, there was more than a full week's supply of food in the house.'

'That's not to say she hasn't looked in when we've been out to make sure we're well stocked.'

'We're not sitting out a siege,' Jimmie answered a trifle scornfully, confident in his own mind that all was well. Anyway it was a chance he'd have to take. He was the one who would get all the blame, not Margaret! He told her so gently as if to make amends for his earlier comment. The reason, anyway, was as good as could be.

Even Aunt Ellen, with her sharpish tongue and house-proud habits, would not like to hear of an animal dying of starvation.

He refused to let his conscience deter him, not even when he heard his sister remark, 'If Aunt Ellen should see us setting off with all that stuff, she's bound to think we're up to something or other and get suspicious.'

Her brother explained more fully what he had in mind. He told Margaret that it was part of his plan to get the very large haversack out of the garage – 'The one we use when we go out for the day with Father,' he said. He intended lining it with some greaseproof paper, and having filled it, hide it in the old summer house just beyond the rhododendron bushes near the gate. 'I'll try and do some of it now while Aunt is still busy,' he murmured. 'Then we can set off early in the morning.'

He could not have spoken at a more propitious moment, for just then a vixen set up a repeated yapping out on the fells.

Margaret, hearing the sound, sensed Jimmie would use it as an excuse. He had a reason for going out again. She found it difficult not to admire her brother's cunning, but still felt inwardly disturbed and very unhappy at the deception they had to adopt in order to look after the dog. They had never done anything so deceitful before.

Jimmie just smiled at her as he quietly left the room. She heard him speaking to their aunt in the kitchen, and after a pause heard the door open and slam shut, and knew he had partly achieved his purpose.

She sat staring pensively into the fire. Watching another log crumble into glowing ash, her mind turned again to the dog on Harter, and she hoped with all her heart that he was warm and comfortable. She had, by this time, convinced herself that what she and Jimmie contemplated doing would surely have met with their parents' approbation were they at home.

Indeed, she had reached a point in her reasoning when she felt their father would have insisted on coming with them on the morrow and try to bring the dog back to the house. Neither John Thornton nor his wife Mary would have been worried by pawmarks on the floor, and hair, perhaps, on the cushions. Aunt Ellen, as far as Margaret knew, was the exception in the family.

With this thought in mind, the sense of guilt vanished, a smile hovering on her face as she thought of her brother doing all the hard work, and hoping their aunt would not find out and put on one of her displays of temper and indignation.

Actually, she had no idea of the really tough job Jimmie was doing. He had thoroughly cleaned out the old large rucksack, and lined it with clean grease-proof paper. Next he took a very large and sharp meat knife from the drawer and, grasping the icy-cold carcass by the legs, started to slice down from the neck, the sharpness of the knife making things easier than he had expected. Within ten minutes, large slices of the lamb were carefully wrapped up in the paper and put into the rucksack, together with a tin of preserved fish which he knew his mother disliked. He wondered why she had even bought it. His final contribution to the dog's diet was a small tin of hard biscuits.

'Anyway, the dog won't starve tomorrow.' This spoken with deep satisfaction.

He crept out into the darkness, and hurrying around to the front of the house, saw the light from the sitting-room window, but did not stop. He kept to the darkened part of the garden, the rucksack feeling very heavy indeed.

The door of the summer house creaked as he opened it, but the place smelled dry and clean. 'So much the better,' he said under his breath, placing the rucksack on the table ready for collection in the morning.

He realized he had been out of the house longer than he had at first anticipated. Thinking of his aunt's sharp tongue he tried to think up a logical excuse for being so long away. Luck favoured him again. Far over on Bampton Common, the vixen started yapping once more. Almost immediately the dog fox gave his reply.

As he rounded the house he found his aunt standing at the open kitchen door. Without any preamble, she asked; 'Have you been looking for that fox and vixen? They might have cubs.'

'They must be up on the common,' he answered at once, accepting her question as a matter of course.

'You'd better go straight into the sitting room or you'll get your death,' she said kindly, 'and I'll bring you both in some hot chocolate. Where are you off to tomorrow?' she asked.

'We might strike off across the fells to the Ullswater road and get the special bus that's going to Windermere for the sailing trials,' broke in Jimmie's voice before Margaret could answer.

Their Aunt Ellen nodded her head with approval. 'You'll have to get away early,' she warned. 'I forget the time it's supposed to leave Patterdale.'

'We'll be up early enough,' Jimmie replied, carrying on the conversation as if they were really going to Windermere instead of to Harter Fell.

'I'll get your sandwiches ready before I go to bed,' their aunt replied. 'Now off with you both. You've had a long day out.'

Thinking of the arduous journey that lay ahead of them the next morning, he admitted that he and Margaret too were tired. Thinking of all the assistance she had given him over the dog, he felt a great respect for her. A queer pang went to his heart as he thought of the alsatian.

'I wish he were ours,' he muttered, hurrying in to his sister, and sighed heavily, knowing that she too entertained much the same desire.

PART TWO

Companions in the Hour of Need

== 7 ==

There could be no doubt now that spring was well established in Lakeland. The morning was early. Out of the mist the sun had risen above the horizon. Everywhere there was a sense of the world awakening. A cock crowed at Bampton, another answered faintly from Whale in the north. Then surely, from the woodland farther off, came the unmistakable call of the cuckoo – generally a late arrival in the north-west.

Margaret, already awake, had watched the daylight gather, first greying the window over which she had forgotten to draw the heavy curtains, then shimmering with light until she knew the sun was up. She heard the two roosters crowing, but couldn't be sure about the cuckoo. She lay quietly for a few minutes longer, listening intently. Her mind was more settled as she tried to piece together the events of the previous day and assemble them into a pattern that would suit the day ahead. Since Jimmie had done everything really necessary towards the success of their day's expedition, she felt greatly relieved.

As far as she was concerned, there were only a few trivial things for her to do. No sooner had she thought of them than she was out of bed, thrusting her feet hurriedly into her slippers and putting on her dressing gown. She combed back her hair in a hurry before going into the bathroom, moving very silently indeed. Her objective was the medicine chest from which she took a wad of cotton wool, a small round of bandage and a half-full bottle of olive oil, to which she added a little antiseptic. These should help to ease and clean up the animal's wound, she thought, well satisfied with the idea.

She found a little-used toilet bag and thrust the articles into it. Not long afterwards she emerged, washed and looking fresh despite her restless night's sleep. She passed her brother on her way back to her bedroom, and he gave her a cheery grin.

'Everything's going fine, as I said it would,' he whispered.

'I hope the dog's all right,' she whispered back, anxiously.

'He will be,' was Jimmie's passing remark as he made for the bathroom.

Margaret sat before her dressing-table mirror, staring at herself thoughtfully, with an idea that exhilarated her. She considered it from every angle before repeating quietly to herself: 'When Father gets back, I'm sure he'll let us keep the dog if no owner is found for him. He has often said we should have a guard dog about the place, especially since he caught that gipsy stealing from the vegetable garden last year. . . .' She smiled. Her brother was right. Everything was going fine . . . would perhaps be better soon. Margaret's eyes had regained their old sparkle, and hope had replaced despair.

Their Aunt Ellen before she went to bed cut their sandwiches for the day. More than that, she had left them a cold breakfast and some fruit.

'Aunt Ellen is really good at heart,' Margaret said to Jimmie, looking down at the breakfast plate of recently cooked ham.

'She certainly is. She looks after us pretty well.'

His sister made the tea, placing on a tray a smaller cup and pot, with milk and cream to take upstairs to her aunt. Aunt Ellen was awake when she knocked at her door, and smiled gratefully when she set the tray on the small table beside the bed.

'We'll soon be off,' Margaret said after the usual morning greetings. 'We have a long way to go.'

Her aunt shook her head as she replied; 'I wish I could

remember the time that bus leaves Patterdale. Anyway, leaving so early, you should be in good time to catch it.'

Margaret, to avoid making any statement that might trouble her conscience, just nodded her head and kissed her aunt 'Goodbye.'

Sitting up to pour out her tea, her aunt said, 'Take good care of yourselves. You and that brother of yours are my responsibility while your parents are away.'

Margaret closed the door silently, thinking of their own more precarious responsibility to the dog on Harter Fell. She was realizing more acutely than ever how much she and Jimmie were relying on the early return of their parents to help them solve their problem.

Twenty minutes later, with the breakfast dishes washed and put away, the two left the house, Margaret with her haversack strapped securely over her shoulders, Jimmie with his slung carelessly over his left arm. There was a new warmth in the air that had not been in it the previous day.

Margaret revelled in it while her brother, out of sight of the house, had departed for the summer house. She stood straight and was light-hearted. She expanded her chest and drew in the air through half-open lips. The mild breeze ruffled her hair and brought colour to her cheeks. When Jimmie joined her, burdened with a heavy rucksack, he thought how well she looked and once more happy again. Not only that, when she saw the heavy burden he carried she gave a low, teasing laugh, and said he must have cleared out the store pantry and that she would carry his haversack. 'There's not as much in ours as in that,' she concluded, thinking then, for the first time, of the small tin baking dish she had purloined from the bottom of the kitchen cupboard and which was seldom used, but would now be useful for water required by the dog.

They struck off in the direction of the Swindale Beck, Margaret in the lead. Within a short while they left the rough road at the point where another beck joined the main stream. From then on it was steady, laboured climbing to higher ground and the approaches to Gatescarth Pass. Jimmie was already feeling the awkward heaviness of the load he was carrying. One of the tins had somehow lodged itself in the small of his back. On reaching the Gatescarth cart-track, he suggested a rest in order to adjust the rucksack.

His sister readily agreed. They had pushed the pace a bit, and she was breathless. The slope where they rested was smooth and grassy, and Jimmie slipped off the rucksack.

Then they heard what Margaret had doubted when in bed . . . a cuckoo! There could be no mistake this time.

'It really *is* spring at last,' Jimmie remarked.

'You're absolutely right. I felt it the moment we came out this morning,' his sister replied happily. 'What's more, Father and Mother will be back this week. . . . I'm quite sure of that.'

'What? Just because we've heard our first cuckoo?' Jimmie answered.

She shook her head. 'No,' she replied. 'I've a distinct feeling they'll be home this very week for sure.'

Her brother did not attempt to argue with her. He had known so many occasions when his sister's premonitions had been right. She was, he admitted, uncannily sensitive in that way.

Struggling back into his rucksack, he merely said: 'Come on! We must get up to that dog or he'll feel we're not coming today.'

Margaret bounded to her feet at once, and continuing to carry his haversack as well as her own, set off at an even stride, making for the steeply rising ground of the pass with her eyes fixed firmly ahead for the first sight of the precipices of Harter Fell. The rising, bouldered land, ridged, and with long valleys striking away on either side, hid what lay beyond; but they were on the track they had followed the previous day. At one place, Jimmie stopped, pointing out the paw impression the dog had left on soft ground, at another where the animal had dragged his hind leg, leaving deeply scored claw markings.

'I hope he's all right!' Margaret exclaimed anxiously.

'He'll be much better this morning,' Jimmie replied confidently. 'Alsatians are a very tough breed of dog. Look at the work they do on the mountains, searching for lost and injured climbers.'

Sounds carry far in the open country, especially so early in the morning. The dog, having found his leg less painful than the stiffness implied, moved towards the entrance of the cave and stared down the trail along which he knew the children to be coming.

He was out in the open standing under the pyramidal shape of craggy mountain rock, with the sun shining full upon him. The leg hurt a little, but he was able to stand on it. As the children topped the last ridge and approached his tail began to wave in recognition and he barked a welcome. It was then as he lifted his head that Jimmie – not Margaret – saw it, the medallion hanging from the chain collar he had not known existed the previous day when he had held the dog.

Saying nothing to his sister, Jimmie's heart sank, for he knew for certain now that the dog had not been abandoned, but lost! Such being the case, that medallion would surely give all the details necessary to find his owner.

His cherished illusions had vanished. They must certainly help the animal and in the meantime, until the owner was located, look after him. His heart went out to his sister, whom he knew had secretly cherished much the same hopes as he, but the fact had to be faced squarely and without any display of sentimentality. The dog had an owner who undoubtedly had been searching everywhere for him, but had failed to find him due to the difficult nature of the terrain.

8

The dog could not suppress the great surge of excitement that welled up in him at the sight of the now hastening children. They were, he sensed, his one sure hope of finding his beloved master, and the more eagerly he barked, raising his head high in his deep-throated greeting, the collar and disc became completely obscured in the deep ruff about his neck. Only Jimmie knew it was there, but he still refrained from telling his sister. Nor, on reaching the dog and falling on her knees, hugging him to her, did she, like her brother the previous day, become aware of it. She was conscious only of his deep chest pressing against her as her hands wandered over his huge frame; then of him touching her cheeks and hands with his wet nose.

Jimmie was now kneeling beside her, enduring less happily because of his knowledge, the animal's tongue touching his face with obvious joy, his dark eyes shining with happiness. Then he pulled away from the two and limped a few steps towards the beck, looking back to see if they were following. He was anxious to let them witness the progress he had made, with the flank still only a trifle stiff.

They followed and, again close to where he had slain the hare, he lapped the cold, sharply running water.

Margaret was overjoyed. 'He's made a marvellous recovery!' she exclaimed with delight. She had already taken from her haversack the bottle of olive oil mingled with antiseptic, together with the bandage.

'What's that for?' Jimmie asked incredulously.

'It will help to take away the stiffness and cleanse the wound.'

He nodded, glancing quickly to ensure that the collar around the dog's neck was still hidden in the thick fur. It was and he breathed a sigh of relief. Jimmie was dreading the moment when Margaret would discover it for herself, and feeling more strongly than ever now the hopes she had cherished, he was wondering miserably how he could comfort her. She had been a great help in the hazardous adventure. At least, together they had located the lost dog and brought him a measure of solace. That factor alone might help to take away the sting of disappointment she had yet to experience.

The dog stood perfectly still while Margaret set about her task of very gently massaging the wounded flank. Sparkling droplets of water fell from his muzzle where he had thrust it deeply into the beck. She drew him closer to her, putting one arm about his neck while her free hand, holding the thoroughly soaked bandage, methodically moved to and fro to ensure the animal got the greatest relief from her efforts. She was certainly succeeding for the dog, in appreciation, turned his head, thrusting his nose into her wind-swept hair.

It was at this point that the fingers of the hand holding him against her encountered the collar. She searched deeply into the thick fur, her heart faltering in its beating. 'He has a collar,' she whispered to her brother.

Jimmie nodded. 'Yes, I only noticed it as we climbed up to the fell, and didn't want to upset you.'

'Then he has not been abandoned?'

'No. There's an identity disc on the collar also. That was what I noticed first of all when he was barking, but, Maggie, you were so excited. . . .' Words failed him, but she understood.

'It's all right, Jimmie,' she murmured. 'I quite understand.'

Then as if to comfort his sister, he said gently: 'We should have guessed yesterday. He's much too well groomed and cared for to be an abandoned dog. I think he's somebody's pet, and both are looking for each other.'

Margaret agreed miserably, all secret thoughts of perhaps, even now, persuading their parents to allow them to keep the dog, vanishing as if in one harsh, painful blow. Yet, as Jimmie in his heart had hoped, deep down inside her was an indefinable feeling of ease because she and her brother had found the animal at a time of adversity and had been able to bring him comfort and certainly temporary companionship.

Slowly, almost reluctantly, she dug her fingers into the soft fur and turned the collar around until she held the medallion between her forefinger and thumb. It was quite clean and unsoiled like the expensive linked collar. Mechanically she read the inscription:

'Hunter'
Kirkbank, Langholm
Dumfries-shire

On the other side was a Langholm telephone number and the name Duncan Walsh.

'Hunter,' she said softly, rubbing him gently behind the ears. The alsatian responded at once, joy lighting up his eyes at utterance of his name, and his bushy tail waving frantically. Margaret threw her arms about him, saying tearfully, 'So you're called "Hunter"? It's a nice name for a dog like you, and it suits you.' Then on a note of despair she couldn't hide from her brother, she added: 'I shall miss you so very much when you've gone back home with your master.'

Up to now, Jimmie hadn't uttered a word, but the break in his sister's voice brought an overwhelming sense of pity to his heart. 'It'll work out all right, Maggie; Father will most certainly see to that. Meanwhile, let's feed him and perhaps, later, try and find out if enquiries have been made about him. If not, we'll try phoning that Langholm number.'

'Shall we take him back with us this evening?' Margaret asked, with a trace of nervousness in her voice.

Jimmie shook his head vehemently.

'No,' he said firmly. 'That would be asking for trouble. Aunt Ellen will insist on us taking him to the police constable at Bampton, and guess that we deliberately lied to her about going to Windermere.'

'Then he'll have to stay here another night?'

'Looks like it, but we'll set about making him a softer bed.'

'Couldn't we hide him in the summer house?' Margaret suggested thoughtfully.

'We could, but supposing he started making a fuss in the night, and barking at every strange sound he heard?'

'That certainly would be a problem.'

In such a serious manner was Hunter's precarious position decided between them, but with an intuition highly developed amongst dogs of his type, he sensed the doubt that like an ominous cloud hung over them, taking away the joy with which they had earlier greeted him. He whined to express his own distress, but a further hug from them both brought the happiness back into his eyes.

One thing they had mutually decided amongst themselves. As discreetly as possible, Jimmy and Margaret would have to make some attempt to find out if anybody had been enquiring after a similar dog.

The boy cut up some of the meat he had brought with him, and while the dog ate ravenously, they sat beside him eating their sandwiches, each very silent as they ruminated upon the future.

'Need we start making enquiries today?' Margaret asked tentatively of her brother.

A smile quivered on his face. 'Not necessarily,' he

answered, 'especially if your premonition about Father and Mother coming home soon turns out right.'

Margaret did not seem so sure now. Even her brother saw the uncertainty on her face.

'Anyway, it can't be long now,' he said reassuringly, 'and a day or two longer can't do any harm.'

'What shall we do about him today?' Margaret asked her brother, almost mournfully.

Jimmie laughed, causing her to smile in return.

'We'll spend the whole day with him as if he were our own. He can walk, and that olive oil worked like magic on his flank. He'll enjoy being with us, and my guess is we should let him hunt around for a while. He might pick up a scent and lead us to the place where he first got lost. We'd then at least have something to go on.'

Margaret looked extremely anxious, cautiously examining the alsatian's flank which certainly appeared so much better. He walked over to the stream to drink after his meal, and clearly moved with greater ease.

Margaret looked up at her brother. 'I think your idea very good indeed. Now let's see if he has been trained to do anything.'

Shadows were creeping over the great hills of West Cumbria, but about Harter Fell, with its steep precipices, the sun was tempered with a quiet murmuring breeze. The dog having returned from the beck was looking up into their faces as if inquiring their next move. He, like Margaret, didn't want to lose their companionship. The two were packing their haversacks, and then packed the large rucksack containing the remainder of the alsatian's food. All three were secreted in the cave, and the animal knew with relief and certainty that they were all going to return later.

Unencumbered, and feeling free, the children stood under the immense rock, with the dog beside them. All three were looking out over an endless upheaval of fells and dales, with many a lake and tarn hidden from sight.

Hunter was full of excitement. He could scarcely keep his feet still. Having known nothing but kindness all his life, he trusted the two children implicitly. Being thoroughly domesticated, and above all, the specially chosen companion of his master who, to him, appeared to possess all wisdom, he expected the children to display, to a lesser degree, the same sort of knowledge. Nor was he entirely disappointed, for Jimmie, with a sudden remembrance of how the handlers of the mountain rescue team gave commands to their dogs – all alsatians like Hunter – said abruptly with a note of authority in his voice; 'Seek!'

The dog, long since obedience-trained by his master, knew the meaning of the word, but lost as he was he did not know quite where to begin, but the word of command had awakened an obscure instinct in him, giving rise to a way of calculating direction now that he was no longer worried and had greater confidence in himself.

His more recent memory of the hare he had slain for the collie roused yet another more distant reflex in his canine consciousness. He knew he had hunted, with great excitement, a similar creature uphill to this place of the big rock, and therefore to obey the boy meant going back to where he had first allowed the animal to distract him. Already he had searched for many days without success, but now Hunter experienced less panic and was capable of applying himself to the task with greater assurance, having the support of the two children behind him.

Filtering through his mental vision was the track up which the children had come. He had come up that same track the day he was lost, and before that had crossed over ridges and hummocks.

Jimmie was watching him through half-closed eyes, and although he had expected an immediate response to his word of command, he kept silent, realizing the alsatian was trying as best he could to think back . . . even to remember.

At that very moment, Hunter's eyes were roving over everything in sight, and an image was forming in his canine brain, seizing for an infinitesimal instant the old vision of the small lake with the clump of pines on the opposite shore, and his master busily sketching. He was gaining a sense of direction through calmness of mind.

When Jimmie finally repeated the word of command, the dog's response was spontaneous. He raised his tail to the level of his back, and moved downhill in a northerly direction, going instinctively along the track Margaret and Jimmie had taken to reach Harter Fell.

'He's no fool,' Jimmie said to his sister. 'He's had some sort of training. Although he's not using his nose, some remembered incident is aiding him. Best let him have his head and follow him.'

Hunter's action was less restricted; he still limped a little, but his muscular co-ordination became very much easier with every yard he covered in spite of the many occasions when the ground was rough, stony and badly rutted. One further revelation was granted him. Although for days now he had tried to find his master, his brief period in the wild, bringing him greater self-reliance, had also given him a new advantage he had not possessed before. He was judging time and distance more accurately. No longer was he wandering aimlessly.

It came almost as a shock to him when he recalled vividly that at the point he had now reached with the scent of the first hare growing cold he had picked up that of the second which caused him to double back in his tracks, and brought him back to the yawning jaws of Gatescarth Pass. He knew he had come here before in his wanderings, but from this angle the whole prospect was different.

Here he paused, his head held high as his nose tested

the air currents. The wind was trickling in from the west and to his great joy there was a familiar scent in that breeze – a scent of resin from trees he had known before. Yet they were not really too great a distance from Harter Fell. It was the breeze that was his ally that day. Then Hunter looked around at the children, and they saw at once a puzzled look in his eyes. Jimmie thought, half murmuring, 'It was here he lost his master, or somewhere near the pass.'

'Do you think he's on to something?' Margaret asked anxiously.

'It could well be, but we're only guessing. Anyway, he appears to know this place.'

Margaret was silent for a short while, staring across the unending fells, broken only by the far-off glint of Hawes Water. Then she said: 'Perhaps some scent in the breeze is telling him something we don't know.'

The sudden light in his eyes at her suggestion told Margaret that she had mentioned a fact he should have known himself. 'That's it!' he exclaimed impulsively.

'It wasn't far from here that we heard the shot that wounded him,' his sister said reflectively.

Jimmie shook his head.

'No, I'm sure that was farther away.' His voice faltered as he looked around. 'Nobody could be sure on that point. These fells and dales all appear alike, and we were resting on a grassy bank.'

His sister couldn't quite make up her mind as to how far they really had been from this place. Jimmie was right when he said all the fells and dales looked alike, but Hunter was undoubtedly on to something. Of that she was more than sure.

Then, as if to give credence to her thoughts, the alsatian began to move off south-westerly, proceeding into a narrow valley fed by a stream that drained into the lake. He was keeping well to the left bank of the tiny beck, quickening his pace, his nose now close to the ground.

Margaret and Jimmie hurried after him. It seemed in his eagerness the alsatian was no longer aware of the stiffness of his flank. His gait was almost normal.

Suddenly the valley took a steep dip, then widened abruptly before what appeared a bowl of blue water with a clump of dwarf pine on the opposite bank. Here Hunter stopped, his nose again testing the atmosphere, scenting more strongly the smell of resin. Every memory of that first day here with his master passed with unusual clarity through his canine mind. Other events too were crowding

in on him, even the way they reached his hidden spot in the dales.

Hunter went into action. He began to cast around with renewed eagerness, uttering inarticulate whines, but with his tail raised and his ears firmly erect. His nose searched diligently every clump of heather and grass, halting at last at a spot where appeared two small holes with four others nearby as if a stool had been placed there and sat on.

Hunter had discovered the place where he had last seen his master. Even now the man's scent lay heavily on the ground, almost suggesting that he had returned to this place many times during the last few days.

Hunter had undoubtedly succeeded in what had, at first, appeared a never-ending quest, but to his great disappointment there was no stool, no easel, and no master!

He barked loud and long, as if to attract the master he had lost, but the sound only echoed over empty, hump-backed hills. Nobody replied, nor did anybody appear on the skyline in response to that call of a forlorn heart.

Margaret knelt before the dog, putting her arm around him and saying as she hugged him close against her: 'We'll find your master for you. . . . We really will. . . .' Her last words were a whisper on an intake of breath.

9

Hunter himself decided on the next course of action. He struggled free of Margaret's embrace, and sniffed long and with serious intent around the four holes where his master had set up the stool for his sketching. The scent here was strong enough to indicate to his canine mind that his master had revisited this place many times, even quite recently. He then did what to the children was the unexpected. Turning quickly, he loped back along the narrow defile with its tiny beck, stopping once where a bootmark on the opposite side made a blurred impression. Around the indentation were strewn a number of spent matches, as if the man who had made the mark had stopped there to light either a cigarette or pipe. Jimmie thought it likely to be the latter and began to build up in his mind a mental likeness of Hunter's master.

Hunter did not pause again near Gatescarth Pass, but pressed on, using his nose all the time.

The children were following excitedly. They did not know what to expect. Perhaps Hunter's master was coming back again in an effort to find him. Both noticed there was an attitude of determination about the dog now. He seemed sure of himself; moreover, they could not fail to see that he had apparently forgotten the flank wound. Either that or the compound Margaret had used had taken away all pain and stiffness, although there was still a slight limp discernible in his loping.

Jimmie had already formed his own conclusions, and they were not far from the actual facts. He felt the alsatian had been enticed up the pass by a rabbit or fox and become totally lost in the fold of the fells. It was more than possible that he had been brought to the small lake from a point near the head of Hawes Water below Mardale Common.

'The old cart-track,' he shouted to his sister. 'That's what he's making for.'

Margaret was now becoming breathless, for Hunter was loping at a quick, swinging pace. 'You could be right,' she managed to gasp. They were long out of the depression by this time and climbing steadily, finally reaching a place they had never visited before. It was a small plateau overlooking a narrowing inlet at the head of the lake. On one side there was bracken searching its way into a clump of woodland, and to the surprise of the children the cuckoo called out once again, this time from the wood itself.

'I knew it was going to be a lucky day!' Margaret exclaimed rapturously.

'Only if Father and Mother are home or on the way back,' her brother reminded her sombrely.

Before she could reply, Hunter was casting about the plateau. Well cropped though it was by rabbits, he was not deterred by any hunting instincts from what was now his sole purpose. He definitely was now searching for something very important to him.

Hunter moved across the small stretch of even ground, and there, petering out along the inlet of Hawes Water, was the end of the old, badly rutted track. The alsatian went hastening down to it, the children stumbling after him. Here he started using his nose more diligently than ever before, coming to an abrupt halt where tyre-marks scored the moist ground. The indentations were numerous, as if a car had been brought to this place many times, and Jimmie, observant as usual, made special note of the footmarks in the soft earth, and the number of burnt-out matches. Hunter's master without question, he thought.

In such a manner was a major piece of Hunter's lost

history put into the puzzle by the dog himself, leaving the rest to be solved as best they could by the children themselves.

The track, nearly always muddy, was never used by the children, but they knew that in following the eastern bank of Hawes Water it eventually became part of a reasonably good road leading to Bampton.

'Shouldn't we make enquiries at the village?' Margaret suggested hesitantly. 'Tomorrow, perhaps?'

Jimmie pondered the idea for a few minutes, feeling again the distress of the man who had lost his dog and was searching for him in vain. Then, not so much out of selfishness for himself, but thinking only of his sister, he answered slowly and thoughtfully: 'We could do, of course, but perhaps when we get home tonight we shall have news of Father and Mother returning. Father would be the best person to help us. He'd know just what to do.' Then as an afterthought he concluded: 'I'm sure there's not been any visitors in Bampton up to now ... certainly no man with a dog like Hunter. We'd have heard all about it in the village if there had been.'

Once more Margaret had to agree with the logic of Jimmie's reasoning. In a place like Bampton, news travelled fast so they certainly would have heard if a visitor was in the village, especially a man with an alsatian dog. In addition, their own home at Rosgill was no great distance away, and all local news was general knowledge within an hour or two. More important to Margaret's view-point, their Aunt Ellen would have been the first to warn them of a missing dog on the fells. Possibly Hunter's master had been staying at one of the more fashionable places in the district, and as Jimmie said, their father would be the very person to help them. . . . At this point, Margaret's thoughts were inclined to wander as she tried to imagine what it would be like with no dog to look after. Perhaps after this, their father and mother might let them have one, if not an alsatian, then perhaps a border collie.

In the meantime, it was clear that Hunter had lost the trail he had, up to this point, been following with assurance. It ceased where the car had been parked; but the dog had far from lost hope. He sniffed the foot prints and match sticks, and from his thorough investigation knew without any error of judgment that his master was still looking for him and would, he sensed, continue the search until he had found him.

* * *

That uncanny instinct all dogs possess in common with all creatures of the wild reassured him on that fact. It was only a matter of time, for him, worked out by day and night, before they met again. The scent trails were all so recent that Hunter knew his master was still in the district. For the time being he would remain in the vicinity of Harter Fell, happier now because of the children's support and his confidence that they would not desert him.

One morning, of this he was more than sure, he would see a familiar figure in tweeds and with a deerstalker cap on his head, walking up the rutted road, and hear as plainly as he heard the cuckoo now the well-loved voice calling 'Hunter! . . . Hunter!' His eyes sparkled and he waved his bushy tail, puzzling the children even more because they did not know what was in his canine mind. To the alsatian, however, it was all so clear and real. He had no doubts now. He knew what they did not – the enduring bond of mutual trust and friendship that existed between himself and a man.

'You'd think he'd be bitterly disappointed,' Jimmie said.

'Perhaps he'd rather be with us than with anybody else,' Margaret answered hopefully.

Her brother refused to accept this possibility. 'No! He's found a positive clue which was missing before, and does not feel quite so lost. I've heard that alsatians are one-man dogs, and Hunter just now is more hopeful of being found by his master. In fact,' and Jimmie spoke very seriously indeed, 'Hunter today has learnt something and knows what we don't.'

Margaret was more puzzled than ever. Although she understood well enough much of what Jimmie had been saying, his final comment was a little beyond her comprehension.

'What *can* he know that we don't?' she queried.

Jimmie pointed to the cart-tracks and the burnt-out matches. 'He knows more definitely that his master is still looking for him.' His reply was uttered quickly as he realized that the dog regarded that morning's trek as very momentous to him. He had found the place where his master had returned on more than one occasion to look for him.

Feeling there was nothing further they could do for the time being save make a few discreet enquiries, they spent the rest of the day wandering around the banks of Hawes Water, Hunter, after being reluctant to move far from the tyre-tracks and footmarks, keeping the place well in view. He kept looking back and twice loped to the track to stare along its undulating course, listening for the beat of a car engine, but there was only the silence of the fells and the gentle lip-lapping of the waves on the shore-line.

The sun was losing its heat as it sank westward, and long strands of purple cloud, touched here and there with a hint of primrose, warned of the approach of evening. Margaret and Jimmie, after spending the whole afternoon by the lakeside, finally turned their faces towards Gatescarth Pass and Harter Fell. On reaching the grassy plateau, Jimmie drew from his pocket a variety of nondescript articles, including a penknife and a piece of tough cord. To his sister's amazement, he proceeded to cut from the edge square-shaped pieces of turf. 'This will make Hunter's bed softer tonight,' he said in reply to her look of enquiry.

In the meantime, Hunter had gone to the other side of the tract of rabbit-bitten grass to stare down at the broken roadway along which his master had driven his car on the first day when they visited the small lake. He remained perfectly still, his head set in one direction, his ears smartly alert. There was still no sign of either car or man, but he did not despair now. Confidence had returned to him, and nothing could shake it. Those very recent footprints told him all he wished to know. His master was still in the district, which knowledge gave him a measure of comfort over temporary disappointment.

Jimmie whistled the dog, who came trotting back at once, and together the three went through the pass and were soon climbing the steep trail to the Fell.

For the dog there was to be yet another night alone in the cave, but the day was not far distant when he was sure the outcrop would be no more than a troublesome memory, carrying with it the affection of two children who had helped him and had been companions in his loneliness.

In less than a quarter of an hour the cave had been transformed by the new soft bed of turf for Hunter, who showed the liveliest of interest in the proceedings. After feeding him once more, Margaret filled the purloined baking pan with water which she placed carefully in a corner should he want a drink in the night. The children then prepared to set off for home. The dog had settled down and was licking his legs and paws, sparing a brief touch of his tongue for the children as they bent over him whispering they would be seeing him again in the morning.

They could see he was more content, no longer fretted by an overwhelming sense of loss.

*   *   *

Back in the grey-stoned house at Rosgill, Margaret and Jimmie Thornton slept snugly in their beds despite the earlier excitement that had so stirred and activated their minds. A letter had been received from their father saying he and his wife were on the journey home and could be expected before the end of the week.

Both children experienced a spasm of regret when they finally came to terms with the stark fact that their relationship with Hunter must soon end. Neither doubted but that their father would very quickly cause enquiries to be made and that the elusive Duncan Walsh would be located and united with his dog.

Whilst they were happy for Hunter, neither brother nor sister could deny that he had won his way into their hearts, but that day's events showed that the alsatian himself had but one objective – to find his master.

In the meantime, until they had their father's advice, Margaret and Jimmie still had a duty to protect and be companionable to the animal.

Before they went to bed, their aunt asked if they would like to have a change from their recent routine by coming with her on a shopping expedition to Penrith. 'It's my last chance before going back to Scotland,' she explained with satisfaction in her voice. 'I'm going by car with the Londesleys of Bampton. It would be a change for you from another day on the fells,' she concluded.

Still with Hunter very much in mind, both children shook their heads. 'We'd much rather be out of doors on the fells for most of our time is spent at school,' was the answer she got.

Thinking of her own schoolchildren back home, Aunt Ellen knew only too well the truth of this statement, and nothing more was said of the suggestion.

Some two hours or so after midnight a dark shape emerged with caution from the cave on Harter Fell. Hunter having awakened suddenly, did so with a keen awareness of all that had taken place during the previous day. He moved off down the trail, treading with extreme care. He knew exactly where to go, knew exactly where and how he had been confused when he had returned to Gatescarth Pass from a different direction after coursing the hare. Because of his recent return to the scene with the children, so many things had become clearer in his canine consciousness.

His eyes, becoming quickly accustomed to the starlit gloom, saw every obstacle in his path; moreover, to his delight, he found himself loping with new-found ease, the lotion Margaret had applied to his flank not only taking away the last of the sting of gun-shot, but most certainly making his leg flexible again so that on level ground he was able to run as of old, in long easy strides.

In no time he had reached the small plateau, sniffing the spot where Jimmie Thornton had cut out squares of turf for his bed under Harter. He waved his tail at the memory, understanding only too well that both children had done so much for him. Ultimately, because he had all the night before him, he investigated again the narrow defile with its tiny stream until reaching the steep dip he stood before the lake that, by day, appeared like a hollow of blue water according to the colour of the sky but that now, at night, quiet and unruffled, seemed like a shapeless mirror reflecting the hard brilliancy of the stars.

Turning away from the lake he made his way to the old cart-track, sniffing the bootmarks where the car tyres had left their impressions before sitting back on his haunches and uttering a broken whine. Still, he was not so disheartened as he had been a few days before.

To the rear of the cart-tracks was the strong scent of the children. Although he did not know it, on their way home they had followed the cart-track to the foot of Mardale Common, reaching the hotel that marked the beginning of the fairly good road to Bampton. Leaving the road, they took a side track away from Hawes Water that would bring them nearer home than by going to the village first and then taking another road to Rosgill.

Hunter was intrigued. Using his nose once again, he followed the children's steps, halting at the hotel for a few seconds only to see if it or the surroundings contained any clues to his master whereabouts. After a general sniffing around, there was nothing he could identify with the man he sought, although two days before he had stopped at the hotel for news of his dog. Unfortunately for Hunter, he had not stepped out of the car, but had enquired of the porter who was engaged in outside chores. That was one of the days when he had left the hard-surfaced road to go on up the rutted laneway to finally stand beside his car calling the alsatian and smoking ceaselessly at his pipe. He, like Hunter, was confident that soon they would meet up. Duncan Walsh, in his anxiety for the alsatian's safety, had alerted most of the district, and had also visited the police, soliciting their aid in the quest.

Meanwhile, Hunter's curiosity, still governing his actions, caused him to continue following the children's scent, and he came at last to the house where they lived. He saw it as a dark mass against the moonlit sky, and went a little way up the drive. Just past the rhododendron bushes that concealed the summer house, he stood trying to discern its special features in the gloom. He saw the starlight reflected on the upper windows, and knowing now where they lived, he felt a certain satisfaction at the knowledge. He knew where he could find them if the necessity arose.

Because of his restlessness that night and moved by an ever-increasing desire to find out more about these northern fells, he trotted slowly up the road until he stood at the outskirts of the village. The house he halted before had a notice board set up inside the gate. It was the home of the local police constable, and although Hunter glanced up at the board, shining white in the gloom, he saw it contained an announcement, and little realized that it was details of himself together with his picture.

It was headed simply:

FIFTY POUNDS REWARD

Folk passing by would have thought it a lot of money for an alsatian. The description given of him also contained the words 'German shepherd dog'.

This was as far as Hunter intended going, and he turned away from the notice board containing his likeness and his value to his master, and headed back to Rosgill and thence along the road to the lane and the long uphill climb to the cave under Harter Fell.

11

Oblivious of the enquiries being made as to the whereabouts of Hunter, and the notices displayed in the locality, the Thornton children set off next day for Harter Fell, happy in the knowledge that possibly on the morrow their parents would be home. Their Aunt Ellen was up and away early, looking forward to her shopping expedition in Penrith. She also was happy and, for once, feeling carefree, arriving at the Londesleys' house in Bampton which was but a short distance from that of the local constable's with its display board which she scarcely noticed, and indeed would not have looked at but for the chance remark of Mrs Londesley that somebody must have a heap of money to throw away, offering a reward of fifty pounds for an alsatian lost on the fells. Before the end of the day she had heard the full story as told by the constable himself to the Londesleys, and was as impressed as the rest of the folk in Bampton at the high figure of the reward.

Jimmie and Margaret were determined to spend the day with Hunter searching for further clues, but both knew it would be only a half-hearted attempt in wandering over ground chosen by the dog himself. 'He must have some idea as to the lie of the land now,' Margaret heard her brother mutter to himself. Although she did not answer, she had the feeling that he was probably right in the assumption.

A mist of rain had blotted out the Cumbrian Mountains, but soon passed over. Jimmie, using his field glasses, focused them on the entire escarpment, picking up first the other Harter Fell above Eskdale, then letting his range of view widen until he was able to pick up clearly Scafell Pikes and Stye Head on to Great Gable itself where still a little mist hung in wreathing vapour. Beyond Red Pike he followed the passage of cloud shadows scurrying quickly over Crummock Water.

'I don't think it's going to be such a good day in the west. We could get rain later,' he said, lowering his glasses.

'Well, it's hot and sunny here,' his sister replied, looking up at the sky with a critical eye.

'Let's hope it remains that way.'

By now they were toiling up the track to Harter. They did not speak, for they were finding the going very heavy that morning for a reason they could not define. At the backs of their minds was the knowledge that not many times more would they come this way, and although they did not realize it, a little of the enthusiasm they had previously experienced had been taken away.

Not for much longer would they have Hunter as an incentive, and they knew instinctively they would be very lonely without him; but they had accepted the fact he belonged to somebody else who wanted him very much, and that he too was aware of it.

Jimmie was thinking that the dog was curiously intuitive, and secretly marvelled at the ways of the animal world.

They fully expected to find the alsatian waiting for them as they approached the precipices of the Fell, but he was not visible. Fear immediately attacked the hearts of Margaret and Jimmie, each thinking that in the night the dog, following up the clues he had already discovered, had gone to pursue further his search for his master. What shall we do now? Margaret thought wildly. We'll never find him unless we wait here for his return . . . that is, if he ever does come back.

Jimmie, who had hastened his steps and was ahead of her, crept up to the narrow vent in the rock face that gave entrance to the cave. As he looked in, creeping forward on bended knees and making no sound, Hunter, newly awakened after his night's adventures, raised his head, whined softly and thumped his tail on the turf. An instant later, he scrambled to his feet, his whines turning into yelps of joy which Margaret heard with relief as she joined her brother in the cramped quarters of the cave.

Hunter nudged Jimmie's hand, looking at the rucksack eagerly. 'He's telling you that he wants his breakfast,' Margaret said.

'We used the last of the meat yesterday. Now it will have to be the canned stuff, and I'd better get to work with the opener on my knife.'

He set to work on the can of meat, watched with great interest by Hunter who had never seen him do it before. It was a bit of a struggle at first to get a hole in the lid and another to cut into it. He finally succeeded, and chunks of juicy, preserved meat fell out on to the empty drinking pan Margaret held before him. There was a jellylike substance surrounding it, and the smell roused the dog's gastric juices and he panted in his eagerness to eat. 'He's going to enjoy this,' Jimmie remarked. 'It's a change from what he's been having, and it certainly does smell good.'

Margaret could not restrain the laugh that bubbled up as it were from her throat. It sounded a trifle rueful, her brother thought as she replied: 'I wonder what Mother and Father would say if they could see us now, using up their store provisions, and Mother so particular when buying canned food.'

'Approve, of course, in the circumstances,' was the ready answer, Jimmie, like his sister, feeling in his heart that it would not be for much longer they would enjoy feeding Hunter. 'I shall hate it when he's gone,' he blurted out suddenly.

He felt his sister's hand on his arm in sympathy. 'So shall I,' she whispered, thinking once again how much the animal had become part of their everyday existence.

She forgot her brief spasm of despair as Hunter ate the meat with the utmost display of relish, licking the pan over and over again until not a sign of food remained. He then moved past them slowly, going to his usual place at the beck and drinking with vigour. As the water was running low because of lack of rain, he stood in it as he drank, enjoying the feel of the rippling coolness about his legs. Even that roused some ancient memory in him, making him tarry longer than he otherwise would have done.

Amidst the obscure sense of conflict in him, Hunter was conscious that but for the fact that whatever happened he must be united with his master, he could, in time, enjoy living like this. Even so, with a deeply rooted awareness of mingled loyalty and affection, he knew he would only be truly happy with the man he had known all his life. At that very moment, the feeling of belonging persisted so strongly in him that he felt an intimate part of Duncan Walsh, and it seemed as though the man himself was but a stone's throw away.

Jimmie and Margaret Thornton also had a place in his heart, but this was due mainly to their coming to him when he was hurt and dejected, and not deserting him. With the uncanny instinct of his kind, as he returned to them, wet from the beck, he knew he would be seeing them frequently in the future. His master would see to that!

For the present, the children were thinking how best to spend the hours they had left with the dog, and decided their first unuttered idea was best – to let the dog wander at will in search of the man to whom he belonged.

After they had rested a while, and Jimmie using his field glasses once again reported that the Cumbrian Mountains were clear of cloud and rain, Margaret nodded with satisfaction. 'I knew it would turn out all right,' was her only comment, putting her arm around Hunter and letting her fingers wander through his fur.

'His legs are a little wet,' she announced.

'He ought to be groomed,' her brother remarked, pulling a steel-toothed comb from his haversack.

The dog recognized the type of article the boy held, and wriggling free of Margaret stood quietly before Jimmie while the boy went methodically about his task with great skill. He knew exactly what he had to do.

In no time at all he succeeded in combing out of the alsatian's fur the many sheep ticks he must have picked up during his wandering over the fells, which had been a source of discomfort to him, and then proceeded to apply his unexpected talents to a general grooming. For his part, Hunter enjoyed every moment of it, especially the feel of the steel teeth along the spine and over the ribs. Jimmie finished off the job by running his hands briskly over the animal's body, realizing then how splendidly proportioned the dog was. After a quarter of an hour or so, he stood back a few paces surveying his handiwork, and saw that the brisk combing and the smoothing of his hands over the alsatian's form had brought back the softness and gloss to the fur so that it actually gleamed in the sunlight.

Now the children saw Hunter as he really was, an alsatian of refinement and selected breeding. He's no ordinary dog, Margaret thought, looking at him in admiration. As if fully conscious of their appraisal of him, he had taken up the 'show stance' as taught to him by his master, and the slope of his back in relationship to his hind quarters, together with the steady uplift of his ears on the truly magnificent skull, not only increased their admiration, but caused them to stare in wonder. Never before had they seen an alsatian so beautiful.

'He's so different from the dogs used by the mountain rescue team,' Margaret murmured. 'He has something they haven't got.'

'I imagine he's a show dog of selected breeding. Anyone can see he's used to being exhibited by the way he stands,' her brother replied after a moment of consideration.

Warming to his theme of which he actually knew so little, Jimmie went on: 'He's been trained, too, like the mountain rescue team dogs . . . not to do the same work, but something else. We found that out yesterday. He acted like a police dog in the way he picked up his master's scent, but he's been more of a pet than a working dog. That master of his must have taken great care of him. That's why they are both searching for each other. . . .' Unable to restrain himself, he blurted out: 'They're almost like one person, each living for the other. . . .'

He then said, in a shamefaced manner, 'Sorry, Maggie, but it's true, you know.'

He heard her whisper, 'I know it's true, but I shall miss him very much when he's gone.' Then loudly and with a stubborn determination in her voice, she added: 'We must persuade Father to let us have a dog. . . . An alsatian too.'

Jimmie grinned at his sister's sudden display of spirit before saying, 'He might agree to a border collie . . . but an alsatian . . .?'

He shook his head.

By now, Hunter had got tired of posing for their admiration and sensed their minds were now engaged in something different, and looked wistfully down the slope, anxious to renew his quest.

The children took the hint, and a few minutes later, with the dog leading the way, they retraced the steps they had taken the previous day. Hunter was full of enthusiasm, intent on following up the discoveries he had already made. He wanted but one further sign to help him, and that in what direction he should go from the lane. One thing he had found out, and that to him was important. He knew without any hint of doubt that he had been brought up that rutted cart-track in the car by his master, and that the man had come there again, and recently.

As Hunter saw it, there was only the possibility that in that narrow old cart-track would be the car once more, and leaning against it, perhaps calling his name, he whom most of all people in the world he sought. This picture was so clearly impressed on the dog's inner consciousness that he almost expected it to turn out that way, but when it didn't, he still was not despondent, and trotted down the narrow valley with its inaudible beck, and finding the hollow of the lake deserted, went casting around the shore-line, stopping occasionally to sniff the scent from the clump of pines on the opposite bank.

Thus was spent another splendid, happy day, with the lake as blue as on that day his master was sketching it. There was always the cuckoo calling and the occasional dipper to hold the attention of the children, but, unfortunately, they had not been entirely unobserved.

12

The gipsy on his way back from Bampton, carrying an hessian-made sack on his back, was an ill-clad, unshaven figure whom nobody in the village had welcomed, although he had paid cash for the wares he carried. More than one trader, trying to ignore the smell from the dirty clothes the man wore and that from his half-washed body, did discreetly wonder where the man had got so much money. Knowing him well by reputation as 'workshy', the more generous-minded of them thought that for once he had broken his rule, and had helped out some hill farmer over by Grasmere where there was a known shortage of labour in the repairing of homesteads that had suffered during the past winter. Many of them, however, felt the most likely explanation was that he had stolen it from some unsuspecting tourist.

In this conjecture the latter were not far wrong. A day or so before, the gipsy had lain sunning himself on one of the fells, listening to the idle chatter of some Lancastrians on a coach tour. The men were in their shirt sleeves, and when the party of eight finally got up to leave, one of the men inadvertently let fall his wallet from an inside pocket as he swung the garment carelessly over his shoulder. Unaware of his loss, he departed with his companions for the road to Windermere where the coach was parked.

The gipsy had waited a few minutes before creeping forward. Once his hand grabbed the wallet and felt its thickness, he knew he was under the eye of Lady Luck that day. He took to one of the dales leading to Stickle Tarn under Langdale Pikes. It was no easy trek he embarked upon, taking him well away from his camping place. He had not given consideration to the distance that day, but only knew he was in luck. The excitement in his mind spurred him on regardless of the uphill climbs he made and the many stumbles caused by broken, scree-scattered ground. He had seemed possessed of extraordinary powers of endurance that morning, and it was not until he was under the enormous shadow of the ominous rock known as Pavey Ark with the tarn at his very feet, that he felt secure and well away from any chance walker or climber.

He had sat for some minutes, breathing heavily like a wild beast, turning the wallet over and over in his hand, curbing his impatience to count the money it contained, but already knowing it was quite a reasonable amount because he could glimpse the edges of the tightly packed notes.

The truth of the matter was that he was, in fact, facing a different sort of problem. Not being subject to sudden outbursts of generosity and knowing only too well the mercenary ways of his wife, he was wondering how best he could arrange to keep the money for himself, save perhaps for a pound or two, explaining that he had earned it honestly by assisting a stranded motorist. Not that she would believe him, of course, but it was the best story he could think of, and in his ears it had the ring of truth in it. He grinned cunningly until he remembered his main problem remained unsolved, and that was where he could safely hide the rest. Thus, he delayed counting the money while he debated in his rather dull mind this weighty and, to him, important matter.

The gipsy was utterly oblivious of his surroundings. He was not afraid of this place as he was of the 'tarn of the raven's rock', and was in no way concerned by the great silence all about him, with the rocky, uptilted defile of scattered boulders and scree rising to the very hem of

Pavey Ark, grim-faced and scarred with countless crevasses of the thousand or more years of storm it had so valiantly defied.

Thinking of his wife, and the idea he had that she possessed the gift of second sight, he hoped she couldn't see him now, sitting in this desolate place with a wallet full of money in his hand.

Impulsively, he pulled the money from the wallet. It was nearly all in five-pound notes and his hands shook with greed and excitement. Wetting his dirty thumb on his tongue, he started laboriously counting it. After a second count, he found it to be exactly thirty-four pounds. He sat looking at it, dazed with astonishment.

Back to the problem of where to hide it. Two pounds of it he would give to his wife, and the rest he had now decided would fit snugly in the old flat St Bruno tobacco tin which he could hide under a rock.

That was one of the few days he could sit back and laugh at his own skill and cunning, thinking himself a very smart fellow indeed.

Extracting the two pounds he intended giving his wife and placing them in one pocket, and putting the remainder very safely in another, he filled the wallet with small stones and flung it as far as he could into the tarn.

Bracing his shoulders resolutely, the gipsy turned away from Stickle Tarn, making off in the direction of Grasmere, intending to avoid it, as he was little liked there, and reach his camp by way of Rydal Fell, and then, with Kilnshaw Chimney as a landmark, struggle over the fells towards the camp.

It was a day to be remembered, his wife accepting without comment the two pounds he said he got for helping a motorist on the Grasmere road. She did not even ask him if he had kept any money back for himself, and looking down at his cracked and broken boots, made her only remark which surprised him. 'When next you go to Bampton, you'd better get yourself a pair of second-hand boots. Just remind me when next you make the visit.'

For the first time he was more than doubly conscious of the thirty-two pounds he had in another pocket, and all but told her when he knew that the admission would only heap words of scorn on his head.

By nightfall, the money was hidden in the St Bruno tobacco tin, which in turn was placed well out of sight in a safe place.

His wife remembered the promise about him getting another pair of boots when, exactly two days later, he set out for Bampton, giving him extra money for their purchase while he had some of his own in his pocket. There was no exultation in his acceptance of it. Although he would never have admitted to such a feeling, he was strangely touched; but he feared the sharpness of her temper had she known the truth. She had listed out as best she could the things she wanted from the village, and presented him with the new hessian sack which she had brazenly taken from under a farmer's nose.

Hence, on the day the children and Hunter were heading for the sanctuary of the small lake, the gipsy, homeward bound, missed them by as little as three minutes. He just heard the young people's voices, and was just in time to witness what he thought could be a dog disappearing behind some hummocky ground. He could not see enough of the dog to determine the breed, and thought, 'So after my raiding the Thorntons' garden, they've now got themselves a dog.' Remembering the threatening manner of the man himself after catching him lifting a few cabbages, he spat out viciously, 'You'd have thought them cabbages gold-dust, the way he carried on.' He paused, resting the sack on the bank beneath which were some heavy wheel-marks of a car.

'Somebody been up here thinking the lane led to some

place and had to turn back,' he said thoughtfully. 'Them tourists are all alike . . . they and their fancy maps.'

He listened intently, but the voices were now lost to his ears.

At last, shouldering once again the heavy sack, and seeking to avoid the inn near Kilnshaw Chimney where he was viewed with great suspicion, he struck away from the head of Hawes Water, crossing the southern slope of High Street, making a detour to reach his camping site a little to the north of the hamlet of Low Hartsop where no trader would deal with him.

They were a pair of good boots, he was thinking, as he felt their bulk pressing into his back. He laughed silently as he recalled how reluctant the old woman had been to accept the three shillings he had offered for them, and they worth every penny of ten. 'They are too tight for my man,' she had said, handing them to him.

From the subject of the boots he was trying to remember a notice he had seen at Bampton, but could not recall what it was. Since he could scarcely read, he had not seen anything but the large type concerning a reward being offered for something or other. . . . One of them Lakeland rescue dogs, he supposed it was. Anyway, the picture on the notice looked like one. That for the present was all he knew.

Great was his surprise when arriving at the camp his wife greeted him with the words that during his absence she had a visit from one of the wardens of the National Park area. He had long been in fear that such a visit was likely because of their camp-fire, but was relieved when told that it was about a dog lost on the fells. He asked whether they had seen such an animal and then gave a warning about the fire. 'Keep it under control,' he said, 'and see that it's out at night.'

The gipsy, having lowered the sack to the ground, suddenly remembered the deer he thought he had shot.

Supposing it were that dog the warden had questioned his wife about? He thought of the notice in Bampton, and for a moment his fear of the law was such that he was ready to suggest they left the Lakeland district and travelled south to his brother who lived near Warrington. Then his wife, who had been examining the contents of the sack, drove the idea from his mind when she expressed pleasure at the purchases he had made, especially that of the boots.

Then during the eating of the food she had prepared his dull mind turned in another direction. If there was a dog roaming lost, he might try finding it and maybe claim that reward he saw advertised. He had succeeded in convincing himself that it was a young deer he had shot at, and missed, so he had nothing to fear. Anyway, he didn't really want to go to Warrington, all factories and streets, and his brother would not welcome him and his wife in the terraced house he had near his job.

No! Best stay here and look for that dog. It might pay off in the end. His mind could cope with only one thing at a time, and no positive memory had he now of the Thornton children and the dog he thought he had seen with them.

* * *

Hunter made no further discoveries that day, but just wandered up and down the lake shore, frequently going to the spot where his master had sat sketching. Once he stood for a long time at the water's edge.

He then relaxed and enjoyed being with the children, who had again brought not only their own sandwiches with them, but more of the delicious meat in the can for him. Apart from the deep fret at times inside him, this life had its compensations. Secretly he was beginning to enjoy it until something made him realize that it was an alien life he was adopting for the present. A little of the joy then went from him, taking with it the sparkle from his eyes, leaving only a troubled sadness.

Jimmie lazily told his sister that they had been very lucky with the weather. 'What on earth would we have done if it had rained most of the time?' he asked.

'Oh, we'd have managed somehow,' Margaret replied complacently.

'We couldn't have taken Hunter home with us,' Jimmie reminded her. 'Aunt Ellen would soon have put a stop to that.'

Indeed, had he but known it, things could well have been different than they supposed. Their Aunt Ellen now knew about the missing alsatian on the fells, and the fifty pounds reward offered for his recovery.

Meanwhile, in blissful ignorance, the children spent a very happy day in that isolated spot by the miniature lake, and during the hours they passed there the sky above was as blue as could be and the sun warm on their bodies while Hunter visited and revisited the tiny holes where his master's sketching stool and stand had been set up. After constantly sniffing around, he rejoined the children and lay beside them as if keeping guard over them.

Only the mewling cry of a buzzard way over on the fells drifted down to them as they half dozed, and always in their ears, but unnoticed by them, the constant sucking of the water on the shore. Now and again the cuckoo called, but his voice too was scarcely an echo in the deep of their minds, as too the infrequent honking somewhere of a raven. Actually, a really perfect day!

Long afterwards, on looking back to that day, Jimmie and Margaret Thornton remembered it as a day of special significance in their lives – a day to be treasured. Apart from the news they heard on returning home, a little earlier that evening, the memory was not dimmed.

Undoubtedly, without any shadow of doubt when that

memory came back to them as so often it did in the trail of startling, quickly moving events that followed over the next day or so, the children held it sacred to their hearts.

Yet it ended as the other days had done, Hunter fed and water left for him and the dog himself contentedly lying on his bed under Harter Fell, and Jimmie and Margaret striding up the drive to the house to find their Aunt Ellen fussing in the kitchen with the litter on the kitchen table which had wrapped the purchases she had made in Penrith.

Her first words on greeting them were, 'Your folks will be home some time tomorrow, and I shall be glad for I wouldn't like anything to happen to you in their absence. Do you know I only heard today that there's a dog lost on the fells, and he might be savage from starvation. Fifty pounds somebody's offering as a reward for his recovery. Fifty pounds for a dog!'

She sniffed with disapproval, thinking of other uses to which the money could be put.

Busying herself with tidying up, she went on: 'I just don't know what the world's coming to when a man can pay that for a lost dog. Now I must get your suppers. I'm thankful you never met up with the beastie while out as you've been these last few days. Anything could have happened....'

Jimmie and Margaret, with the thought of Hunter's gentleness warm in their hearts, smiled self-consciously, then expressed their joy at their parents' imminent return, while their Aunt Ellen went on repeating, 'Fifty pounds' reward for a dog, and he one of those alsatians forbye....'

Margaret nearly blurted out: 'And he's worth every penny of it', but held her tongue, knowing that whatever happened now, Hunter would soon be with his master.

When she went to bed that night she stood as she often did staring out of the window. In spite of the ache in her heart at the thought of losing Hunter, she managed to say huskily: 'Sleep well. Soon, quite soon now, you and your master will be together again, for my father will be home, and he will surely help. Sleep well, Hunter.'

Earlier that evening, at about the same time the children were on their way home, two cars were approaching the border, one with John and Mary Thornton heading for Rosgill, and another – an estate car – coming from Langholm with Duncan Walsh at the wheel heading back to the lakes, accompanied by another alsatian, who sat quietly in the rear of the vehicle. This dog, a magnificent black-and-tan animal, was Hunter's younger half-brother. He had the distinction of being one of the best tracking and obedience-trained alsatians put in the trials for the breed, and had been awarded many cups and prizes for his highly regarded performances. He was a dog that in alsatian circles was known as a 'good all-rounder', and showy at that.

Later, at a motel in Carlisle on the south-bound road, both cars were parked side by side, but when the Thorntons came down next morning, the other had gone, the driver saying he wanted to leave very early and being the first man down to breakfast. 'He seemed in a great hurry to me,' said the waiter, serving the other guests who also were down early.

'Probably wanted to get somewhere quickly,' replied John Thornton, little guessing how soon he and the man with the alsatian were to meet again, and the harrowing circumstances that were to follow the meeting.

His wife smiled. 'We at least can take it easy for the rest of the way. We'll be home long before evening.'

Her husband nodded, returning the smile with affection in his eyes.

PART THREE

Return to the Loch and River

13

On the very day that Jimmie and Margaret Thornton were always to regard as one never to be forgotten in their hearts, and their parents and Hunter's owner were speeding along their respective roads towards the border, news of the fifty pounds' reward being offered for the recovery of an alsatian lost on the fells had, by now, been widely circulated. Herdsmen and small-holding farmers, gathered at the inns of both Penruddock and Troutbeck, were noisy and eloquent in the expression of their varied opinions and, at times, disclosed a threatening attitude towards the dog when discussing him.

Seated at a beer-stained table in the bar parlour of the inn at Penruddock, Jim Mason from Pooley Bridge was arguing with Thomas Burton from Askham, the others, a dozen in all, standing around listening.

'I've lambs below High Street,' Mason was saying angrily, 'and with a dog running loose and doubtless near to starvation point, he could cost me more than that reward.'

Burton replied in his usual quiet manner, 'There's been no report of lambs being molested or found dead up to now. I'm sure every man here will agree wi' me on that.'

The others did not dispute the fact, one even speaking up by saying that the dog was described as a German shepherd, 'and,' he added slowly, as if he knew all about the breed, 'they're protectors of sheep . . . not killers!'

'As I said,' Mason replied hotly, 'this one may well be starving, and it's obvious to anyone that a dog will attack and worry to kill when hungry. Even our own collies have been known to do just that at times. Sheep-worrying by no matter what breed of dog is a serious offence.'

At this juncture one of the Lakeland rescue team men walked in, with an alsatian at his heels. 'Seems like you're the lucky one and found him then?' was the general enquiry.

The man shook his head.

'This is one of our own dogs,' he replied, 'trained to find climbers lost on the hills, and a right good job he does of it too.' Then reverting to the conversation he had overheard, he offered his own personal advice on the matter. 'Whilst every dalesman has a perfect right to look after and protect his own flock, he just cannot go and shoot any dog he finds alone on the fells, especially if he has no proof that the animal has been worrying sheep. If any dog shot under such circumstances should be valuable, the man can be taken to court and damages can be awarded against him.' He was looking straight at Mason of Pooley Bridge as he spoke.

'Ah, hell!' Mason spat out viciously. 'We've our rights. T'wud serve the fellow right who let him wander off the way he did.'

This time, nobody spoke up on his behalf. They were all thinking of the fifty pounds' reward which was better than a possible lawsuit.

It was far better just to keep a look-out for the dog as the Lakeland rescue man suggested, and forget all about Jim Mason's ideas.

At the inn at Troutbridge the subject was on much the same lines. Some of the men feared for their sheep and lambs, but not one of them could claim that any of their flocks were injured or showed signs of having been harassed. Still, a large dog missing on the fells was regarded as a serious matter by one and all.

They jointly came to a more sensible solution to the

problem than their fellow herdsmen and farmers at Penruddock had, at first, been inclined to do. All decided to keep a shepherd with their flocks both by night and day. Moreover, before sundown it was agreed that all sheep should be rounded up and driven to shelter in one of the narrow dales with which the district abounded.

Yet, even as they set about driving their sheep to shelter near their farms, and dusk deepened, one individual lying on a dirty mattress under some old horse blankets lay awake, listening to the night wind fingering the flap of the tent that sheltered him. His wife's inarticulate mutterings in her sleep were too familiar to have any effect on him. Indeed, he scarcely heard them, as, in his own simple way, he forced his thinking into a channel that might support the idea that had entered his mind. That deer he shot at might have been the missing dog. He had thought him a curious shape at the time, and but for the raven's savage attack on him, he could have set off to trail the creature. As it was, he was fairly certain that he had only winged the animal, for he was too far off to be really hit by the widespreading buckshot.

Not for one moment did his thoughts turn to the Thornton children and what he imagined had been a dog with them. Even had he done so, he would have considered the animal their own after John Thornton's threat. It would have been natural for the man to get a dog to protect his property.

He found it difficult to make a strategy of the type that would enable him to explore the fells east of the Kirkstone Pass Inn, and if by chance he was fortunate enough to find the dog, how best to capture him without meeting with injury himself? Thinking of the rescue team dogs, and their uncanny ability of locating walkers and climbers lost and some injured on the Cumbrian Mountains, he muttered to himself: 'Them alsatians be chancy creatures. This one may find me, not him being found by me.

What could I do then if he decided to attack?' He shuddered beneath the blankets, remembering how thoroughly demoralized he had been by the raven's assault on him, and an alsatian was a different proposition from a cringing half-bred collie who went in terror of him.

His mind continued active until the dawn made red the sky and day came stealing over the fells and dales.

Earlier, he had not been the only person in the tent trying to make plans. His wife too had been thinking of the reward money. Fifty pounds seemed a lot to her, and she also had been considering what could be done to catch the dog. She came more quickly to a conclusion than her husband. As she turned over prior to going to sleep, she was thinking what could be better than covering him, if found, in the meshed net she had made months before to trap sea-trout on the outward flow of the Solway Firth. Once it was over the animal's body, if her husband, fool though he was, acted quickly in closing the ends around the animal so he could not escape, they might perhaps succeed in dragging him to Bampton and claim that reward.

As her eyes closed in sleep, her last conscious thought had been of leaving these desolate moors and dales and going back south.

Once she was roused by the rising wind battering at the tent, and her mind, still drowsy with sleep, remembered the plan she had in mind to capture the alsatian. She would question her husband in the morning. He was always out on the fells poaching for the pot, and seldom returned without a rabbit or hare for his pains. He also seemed in luck these days. She vaguely remembered the tale he had told of the generous motorist on the Grasmere road. That was a rare bit of luck, if you like, and he not knowing a thing about cars. She grinned grotesquely over the incident, knowing he had not given her all the money the supposed man had paid.

As she turned over to sleep again, she murmured: 'No doubt he had a pound or two hidden away. He's a cunnin' one, is that feller....'

*   *   *

The children at Rosgill were up quite early and took their aunt a tray of tea and biscuits to her room. She was surprised to see them washed and dressed and looking very presentable.

'My goodness!' she exclaimed. 'Is it that late?' Her glance went to the clock on the bedside table, and she smiled. 'It's only a little after seven,' she said with relief in her voice. 'I'll get up shortly and set everything in order for your parents' return.'

As she spoke, the phone rang. Margaret went hastening out of the room to answer it, leaving her brother standing gazing a little self-consciously out of the window.

Returning a few minutes later, Margaret, breathless with excitement, could not refrain from blurting out, 'They'll be home early this evening.... That was Father speaking from Carlisle. He said that he and Mother would be having lunch in Penrith and perhaps look around the shops. Anyway, they'll be back this evening. Oh! I'm so glad.'

'That'll give me a little time to straighten things up a bit and arrange a fine high tea for you all,' their Aunt Ellen replied. Then abruptly, too abruptly, Jimmie thought, she asked: 'You're not going out today?'

Both, thinking of Hunter, said they would only be out for the morning or until the afternoon. Seeking to retrieve his composure, Jimmie added with a smile that completely allayed any suspicions his aunt might have: 'You've always said you get on better without us under your feet, unless, of course, there's anything special you'd like one of us to do?'

She shook her head. Then she told them to be off and make sure they were back home in time to greet their parents.

The two hastened off with brief goodbyes, causing her to smile and say to herself: 'They're very happy, carefree children at heart . . . Spoilt maybe . . . but certainly happy.'

In this last observation she was utterly wrong. Although normally happy by nature, they were, on this particular morning, very worried children indeed. They were uncertain as to whether or not they should bring Hunter back with them or see their father first and explain things to him. He would want to know why, since the dog wore a collar with an identity disc on it, they had not informed the police instead of keeping him hidden away and feeding him with food taken from the store pantry. To this likely question they knew they had no satisfactory answer. Yet neither doubted that their father would be quite sympathetic in his understanding of their problem, particularly as they had not noticed the collar and disc when they first found the dog hiding in the cave under Harter, being, at the time, more concerned with the injuries the animal had received from a shot-gun.

That, Jimmie explained, was a logical excuse, and true; but when he said quite casually that he had already packed more food in the rucksack, Margaret expressed the utmost alarm.

Wishing to set her mind at ease, her brother said, 'After feeding him, and taking him for a walk over the fells, we can again leave him comfortable in the shelter under Harter and hurry home and explain to Father what we've done. Don't worry, Maggie,' he said gently; but whilst agreeing with him as she usually did, she had to express one major flaw in Jimmie's proposal. 'We know now that his master is searching for him and offering a big reward for his recovery. Aunt Ellen kept on about it last night, and we'd certainly be expected to bring the dog back with us since we know where he is.'

'Best do it my way,' her brother replied obstinately, having overlooked this vital fact. 'Then tomorrow, with Father, we can go up to the fell and bring him down. Father will then do the rest. He'll probably phone that Langholm number. Anyway, we've been looking after the dog until he got back because we weren't too sure what to do.'

'It's plain to me what we should have done,' Margaret answered boldly. 'We should have given up pretending that Father might buy the dog for us, and telephoned Langholm ourselves.'

Jimmie nodded his head moodily. 'You're right, of course, but it's a case of being wise after the event. We did not know of the reward being offered until Aunt Ellen told us last night. Anyway,' he said slowly, clutching as it were at the last straw to support what they had done, 'we had to do something about that wound. Hunter couldn't have walked far with those pellets in his flank.'

This was the one consoling thought he had until Margaret broke his illusions again by saying: 'And we enjoyed being with him so much. He's such a wonderful dog. I'm going to miss him so much when he's gone. . . .'

'Cheer up, Maggie. After this, Father is sure to let us have a dog. Perhaps Hunter's owner will know of one that wants a home.'

Ten minutes later they were making their last trek up to Harter Fell, and from the very moment they left the house, became involved in what turned out to be a hazardous adventure in order to protect Hunter. The gipsy also was setting off for that part of the fells where he had seen and shot what he thought was a deer but had now decided was the alsatian for whom fifty pounds' reward was being offered. He bypassed the inn at Kirkstone and after a stiffish climb to get out of sight of the road was forced to pause in one of the dales to regain his breath. Not many minutes later he was off again, after readjusting the meshed net he had slung over his shoulder in which, with good luck, he hoped to ensnare the dog and claim that fifty pounds' reward money.

The battle of wits between the gipsy and the Thornton children was about to begin!

═ 14 ═

There was a faint haze over the fells that morning, and the sun a shimmering red glow behind it. There had been a fall of dew overnight, and the footprints of animals that had passed over it during the hours of darkness were clearly seen. The breeze that had touched none too gently the flap of the gipsies' tent had gone long before sun-up, and Jimmie, feeling the way up to Harter had never been so long as now, burdened as he was with further supplies for the dog and themselves, remarked breathlessly that when the haze lifted, as it surely would in an hour or so, it would be very warm.

Margaret also was feeling the way up to the fell to be more arduous than had seemed the case on previous occasions, and she was pleased when, after following the course of Swindale Beck, they came at last to the mouth of Gatescarth Pass. When her brother suggested resting up a bit, she readily agreed.

The haze was slowly lifting and already the heat from the morning sun was making the dew sparkle and where a spider had woven a delicate web of lace across a bush of gorse on the final stretch of track towards the fell, the children stopped for a moment to admire the drops of moisture, some glistening with varied colours, others crystal clear.

Until then they had resumed their climb in complete silence, but now Margaret gave an exclamation of delight at the web so beautifully displayed. 'It *is* lovely, isn't it?' she whispered to her brother.

'It certainly is,' he answered loudly, anxious now to get to the fell and Hunter and enjoy to the full what little time they had to be with him. He was impatient to press on and be with the dog for as long as possible.

He little guessed how long that was likely to be. Like Margaret, he expected the last few hours alone with Hunter to pass as quietly as had all the other days they had spent with him, and he would have denied hotly that any sense of premonition had prompted him to replenish well the rucksack he carried on his back.

All this time, Hunter had been lying outside the cleft in the fell, listening and waiting for the children. They were, he felt uneasily, a trifle late this morning, but he never for one moment doubted that they would come. None the less, his wet nose was never still, sniffing and taking in all the scents that came to him on the little spasms of breeze that constantly blew over him. Since all these came from off the Cumbrian Range, they carried, for the most part, the smells of newly flowering gorse and pine-scented water, with an occasional salty tang from off the distant sea. This resulted in him having no firm indication of Jimmie's and Margaret's approach until they breasted the final ridge below the cliffs of Harter, and their voices reached his ears. He jumped to his feet, trembling with eager anticipation.

Their voices were more distinct now, and at last he could restrain himself no longer. With a deep bark that went echoing over the fells, he went racing down the track to be hugged and greeted with enthusiasm by Jimmie and Margaret, who had been wondering if, on this day of all days, he had wandered off on his own.

Jimmie took the full weight of his body as Hunter reared up on hind legs in wild excitement, reeling back a little on his heels because of the rucksack he carried on his back and the uneven ground behind him. It was his sister who aided him in regaining his balance by putting her arms around the dog's neck so that he turned his attention to her. Then, still barking, he swung around, going back up the trail to Harter, Margaret and Jimmie hurrying along after him.

The sound of the deep-throated echoing bark had roused one other – the gipsy, who, in a narrow dale, well away from the lake where the malicious raven dwelt on his ugly rock, stood tense and still, trying to place from which direction the barking had come. No matter which way he turned his head, the recurring echoes misled him, but he had one place very much in mind to visit that morning, and that was Harter Fell, and he still had a long way to go to reach it. Besides, it was getting very warm, and he just had to take a rest. Looking up at the sun, now riding clear of the haze, he was able to determine to some extent the time of day, and he considered he had many hours before him to locate the hiding place of the dog who had been barking. 'He's a big one if I'm any judge from that bark of his.... Huntin' down rabbits, no doubt,' he reflected lazily. 'That'll be all to the good. I might find the fellow with his belly full an' fast asleep....' In a moment or two, he was dozing himself, and soon snoring.

Meanwhile, Jimmie having fed Hunter generously from the meat he had cut from the carcass in the store, saw him look at them both with something akin to affection before going to the beck to drink. He certainly had been very hungry, but it was not because the children had satisfied his need for food that he was aware of his growing fondness for them. It was something more than that. They had become close and trusted companions.

'He's becoming really attached to us,' said Margaret over her shoulder, as she followed the dog to the beck to fill the drinking pan with fresh water. Returning with it held steadily in both hands, she crept into the cave, leaving it in the usual spot where the dog could not overturn it. She then set about smoothing out the fern and moss with which Jimmie had lined the hollow where the dog slept, thinking sorrowfully that it would be the last night he would spend there. Her lowered spirits were only lightened by the fact that night was still far off and they had many hours still before them. As she backed out of the cave on her hands and knees, watched by Jimmie and Hunter, she had a dim, but uncertain impression of her handkerchief, and Jimmie's, hanging from the ledge where they had placed them to dry on that first day of their encounter with the dog when she had squeezed the gun shot from his flank and bathed it afterwards. It was an impression that scarcely touched her memory, and she made no attempt to remove them — one of the many clear indications that at some time or other they had been in that cave with the dog, the pan of water filling in the last of the vital details.

If anybody had left all the necessary evidence behind them, it was these two who, in their innocence, had no idea how it might be interpreted in the near future.

While Margaret sat watching him with interest, Jimmie was wrapping up the remainder of the meat in silver foil to keep it fresh. She then saw with surprise that the rucksack also held more tins of meat and, with amazement, half a loaf of bread.

'We couldn't very well bring sandwiches today,' he said in answer to her look of silent enquiry. 'It would be too suspicious. Anyway, we've to get back home early, but we'll want something to eat during the time we're out with Hunter. Let's just think of it as being on a picnic.'

'You're nothing but a scheming rogue,' she answered with amusement. 'I only hope you'll be able to convince Father and Mother that it's been in a good cause.'

Jimmie became serious, his brow creased as he concentrated on re-packing the rucksack. 'I *have* been thinking about that part of it,' he replied slowly. 'Hunter is one thing they'll readily understand, but taking all that grub...?'

Return to the Loch and River

His sister immediately sought to ease his conscience. 'We're in this together. Remember? Anyway, nobody at home will starve. The kitchen cupboard is full of goodies, with a fresh joint Aunt brought back from Penrith. She certainly intends preparing a very special "high tea" for us all.'

'Then we'd better get on with our walk or Hunter will be disappointed. We really must make the most of today and forget everything else. I have an idea that for a change we make for the Borrow Beck and follow it as far as we can to Shap Fells. We can then eventually swing back in the direction of Harter. It should be an easy walk and one that will take us to that hidden valley near Long Sleddale.'

'We haven't been there for a long time,' Margaret answered eagerly. 'Hunter will like it too. He can run around to his heart's content.'

Hunter had been watching them intently, his tail waving furiously. He somehow sensed that this was truly going to be a day different from the others he had spent with the children.

They set off for the place Jimmie asserted was an easy crossing over the beck above Sadgill. It did not take long for them to leave the precipices of Harter Fell behind and ascend the southern slopes of the much smoother climb to Branstree, reaching the pass in less than an hour with a glimpse of Long Sleddale appearing directly ahead, framed as it seemed between the crags through which the track they followed thrust its way. The sunlight shot arrows of light from the water, and they stopped at the top of the pass to take in fully the whole scene, which finally receded into a finely cultivated valley, sealed off by exceedingly high crags at the upper end.

This respite, forced on them by the continuous climb they had made to a height of over nineteen hundred feet, had left them breathless. They did not sit down, but just stood in the gap of the pass, with Hunter silhouetted against the sunlight. This simple but natural act on their part was the beginning of all the troubles that were to follow. All three made a sharply lined etching against what had become a wispy cloud-flecked sky, with a patch of blue directly above them.

It was the same moment that the gipsy, labouring and swearing softly to himself about the task he had embarked upon, yet remaining dazzled by the money he hoped to get for the capture of the dog, reached Harter Fell. Like the children an hour before, he stood breathing heavily, looking moodily about him. He had hoped to find the dog here, sated with food and sleep, presenting an easy victim to the plan formulated between his wife and himself. He even held the net in readiness. Looking around in bewilderment and uncertainty, he caught sight of the handkerchiefs at the narrow mouth to the cleft in the crags. He immediately dropped on his hands and knees to investigate further. When he emerged from the cave there was a look of vicious triumph on his face, and even *his* slow-thinking mind reached the one and only conclusion possible.

The animal he aimed at and succeeded in hitting with some of the scattered shot had undoubtedly been the missing alsatian and not a young deer as he had supposed. One further thing too was obvious to him now. It was the Thornton children who had found him, and helped him during the period the wound had been troublesome, and the animal himself unable to walk. That pan of water in the corner of the cave seemed proof of that!

As he continued to stare at the entrance to the cave, bit by bit the main pieces of the puzzle fell into place, forming a satisfactory whole in his mind. He felt he knew the entire story now and was galvanized into immediate action.

First he looked down the trail to Gatescarth Pass, but

as he continued to stare, knowing if anybody were making for the pass and Mardale Common on their way to Rosgill they would, at some point, go over the high land south of it, he lost all sense of time. He stood looking over the fells, but there was no movement in that direction, and the only sound was that of a cuckoo calling repeatedly from a long way off. The call irritated him, increasing his sense of frustration.

Harter Fell, rising over two thousand feet above the surrounding hills, was a good vantage point. His cunning mind was darting from one idea to another. Were the children taking the dog home at last because he could now travel without difficulty, having recovered from the wound he had suffered earlier? This and a hundred other thoughts filtered through the gipsy's brain. Remembrance of the day he returned from Bampton and heard children's voices, thinking also that they appeared to have a dog with them, seemed of little importance now that he had made this important discovery in the cave. They couldn't possibly have had the alsatian that day if they had been feeding him and attending to his injuries in this hide-out under Harter. It was more likely they were making their way up to the fell, taking a route other than that by way of the trail from Gatescarth Pass. One other thing crossed his mind. They couldn't possibly have had the alsatian on that occasion, for there was that notice of the missing dog posted up at Bampton, and not knowing of the absence of the Thorntons from home, he admitted that for all his high-handed attitude on the subject of trespass, John Thornton was a just, straight man, and would have notified the police at once of the children's discovery. He therefore inclined to the view that the children had been forced to wait for the animal's recovery from the buckshot before taking him home; and that was today.

This was the ultimate conclusion the gipsy came to at the end of his deliberations; but which way had they gone? That barking he had heard earlier was sufficient proof that the dog was now moving about the fells with the children. He was confident he had reasoned the matter out aright. The Thornton children had been looking after the alsatian and were now taking him home, possibly going to Rosgill by way of Shap to make it easier walking for the animal. Grinning now with self-confidence, the gipsy exclaimed: 'But I'll head them off, and trap the dog in the net. I'm more than a match for a couple of kids. . . .'

He did not reckon on the dog himself.

Once again he had the feeling that the fifty pounds' reward was as good as in his pocket, and he was more than sure of it when, looking east towards Branstree, he saw on the pass the outline of figures against a patch of blue sky . . . and a dog with them. . . .

He shouldered the net and began a hasty scramble in the direction of the smooth slope of the ridge. For a few short-lived moments he felt luck was turning in his favour. Hunter, having glimpsed a man moving up the fells, gave a deep bark, and before either Jimmie or Margaret could check him, he went racing downhill towards the man he had mistaken for his master.

15

He heard the children calling after him, but in his rising excitement their cries went unheeded. They had started running after him, but he was moving so fast they knew they could never hope to catch up with him and stopped. The fellow coming away from the fell was now clearly visible on the first high ridge east of Harter. He was pushing himself hard, stumbling at times, but coming on with a sort of grim determination.

Jimmie in his agitation fumbled with his field glasses, his fingers quivering as he focused the lens on the approaching shape, still some distance off, but sharply defined in the glasses once they were correctly set.

'Maggie,' he said in awe-stricken tones. 'Hunter is mistaken if he believes that man to be his master. . . . It's that terrible gipsy. . . . We must do something . . . and quickly too!'

Even as Margaret's cry of dismay reached her lips, the alsatian had slithered to a stop, his head high as he tested the sudden stream of air coming to him from the west. The hair on his shoulders bristled, and a growl rumbled in his throat. This was the exact moment that the gipsy's supposed lucky break ended, and it was the breeze that betrayed him to the dog. Stronger than any scent of moorland fern and water was the man-musk the alsatian recognized. It had been all around the lake where the collie had been almost drowned, and on the rope to which the rock had been attached, and with the astuteness of his breed, he knew it to be evil. Any disappointment he felt was lost in an awareness of his obligations to the children, and he realized that he must return to them at once and protect them.

So involuntary was the impulse in him that he turned about instantly, loping back to Jimmie and Margaret, who were standing close together a little below the pass. Hunter reached them within a few minutes, running around them and barking, telling them as best he could that the man ascending the hill was evil and dangerous.

Overjoyed at the dog's return, the children responded at once by going back over the pass and disappearing entirely from the skyline – the dog with them.

The gipsy, witnessing the manoeuvre, felt the elation he had experienced ebb from him, guessing exactly what had happened, and this time he was absolutely right in his thinking. Cursing at what now appeared to be his impotence in getting possession of the dog, his mind reverted to other means of separating the dog from the children. He was on the wrong part of the fells to be sure of his actual position and that of the children and dog ahead of him. As he had now lost sight of them, he sat on a hummock and tried to assess the direction the three might take to reach Rosgill by looking back at the cliffs of Harter Fell and then looking up again at the smooth saddle of Branstree. It then occurred to him they might make for the road at Shap, hoping to reach the track beyond the old Abbey and so on to Rosgill.

The more he thought about it, such a course was the most likely one for the children to adopt. Shading his eyes, and looking up at the sun, he endeavoured to take a bearing from its position in the sky. Unfortunately for him, it was approaching high noon and he was quite unable to determine the route he should take. One thing he was certain about, it was of little use pursuing the three by way of Branstree. He would somehow or other try rounding it by way of the Swindale Beck and Ralfland Forest south of Keld.

The breeze that had warned the alsatian of the mistake he had made by leaving the children to run to the man he thought was his master had now become a strong westerly air-stream. There were times when it was quite boisterous, striking in sharp gusts, as, during the night, it had constantly buffeted the tent in which he and his wife lay scheming.

Finally, he set off with the intention of rounding the slopes of Branstree, guessing that by so doing he would eventually come out on the western edge of Shap Fells. By now, he had no direct plan in mind, everything previously having been based on the conviction he would find the dog in the region of Harter.

He trudged on, brooding over his misfortune and at a loss as to what to do next to separate the dog from the Thornton children. It was uppermost in his mind that he would have to move cannily. Where before he had been inclined to regard John Thornton as a just, upright sort of man, he now began to think of him as a potentially dangerous one, particularly where his children were concerned. If they came to harm! The gipsy tried to thrust the thought from his mind, realizing they had found the dog and doubtless helped him when wounded. Not only did this give the children prior claim to the animal, but the dog himself would not be enticed away, and might even prove aggressive if anybody came too near the children.

His frustration grew with every mile he trudged, wondering how it would all end. Nevertheless, he still had every intention of trying to get that fifty pounds, Thornton or no Thornton. Better him, perhaps, than the sharp edge of his wife's tongue. . . .

There were now repeated wind changes, sometimes coming from the west and north-west, then veering without warning to a cold stream of air from the north-east.

The gipsy struggled against the infrequent impacts

from behind and before him, finding refuge at last in the dales where it was close and warm. He was beginning to realize he was no longer young, and that the children and the dog that had gone over Branstree were by now well away from him.

He continued on, working to the plan he had newly decided upon. 'Shap!' he kept saying to himself. 'That's the way they'll go to reach Rosgill.' He knew the dale he traversed rounded the slopes of Branstree, and it would be less than an hour before he came out on to the fells themselves within sight of the Swindale Beck and Ralfland Forest.

Long before this, Jimmie and Margaret were acutely conscious of the danger that might threaten them from the gipsy, but they were now well hidden as the track they followed fell steeply in the direction of Long Sleddale and the remote valley with Grey Crag tarn practically concealed by the eastern precipices of the deeply recessed dale, narrow and straight.

'I think we've shaken him off,' Jimmie said huskily, glancing back over his shoulder, and noticing Hunter was a little to their rear, fully alert and ready to protect them should the need arrive.

'Hunter will not let the man harm us,' Margaret said tentatively. 'I'm sure he'd fight the gipsy if he tried any tricks.'

'I'm sure he would,' Jimmie answered with deeper assurance in his voice.

Once in the valley itself, they were out of the varying breezes and especially that cold air-stream from the north-east.

'I think we're quite safe for the time being,' Margaret said. 'Let's take a rest and have that picnic you spoke about.'

'Yes, I think we're all right now,' her brother replied, glancing back along the track that meandered between the overhanging crags that hid it from Branstree. 'We'll have the picnic, as you say, and afterwards think up a new plan. We daren't take Hunter back to Harter for the night or that gipsy fellow will surely make an attempt to catch him by fair means or foul. . . . I think he would even resort to outright cruelty in order to get that reward.'

Margaret nodded her head gravely before saying: 'We'll think up something new. It shouldn't be too difficult. Now let's see what you've got besides the loaf and butter. . . .'

'It's nice here,' Margaret said, sitting with her back against a boulder, with Hunter close beside her. One arm went around the dog, holding him close against her, feeling, as Jimmie now did, that the one safe place for the animal would be at home. Their father, hearing of the gipsy being out on the fells, would surely approve.

It occurred to her then that her father, who had always regarded the gipsy with the utmost suspicion whenever he chanced to see him in Bampton, would undoubtedly express concern at the encounter, since his own children had found, and were bringing home, the missing alsatian. Apart from that, it would add support to what she and Jimmie would have to tell him. Moreover, as they had no other choice but to let Hunter go back to his owner, it might as well be sooner than later. That, as Margaret saw it now, was the only difference from the plans they had earlier agreed upon.

When they had finished their picnic lunch they lay with their backs supported against a low ridge, for a few minutes, at least, completely relaxed.

Hunter went over to the tarn to drink, and both children had a remote yet fleeting sensation that all this had happened before. It was as though, simultaneously, they were caught up in a dimension of time completely outside themselves. In its most important aspect it was a dimension of utter silence.

Jimmie broke the silence first. 'We've certainly put that gipsy off the scent,' were his opening words, spoken idly and slowly. 'He must have lost all trace of us when once we passed over the summit of Branstree.'

Margaret also spoke as if she had been wool-gathering in her mind. 'I wonder what direction he took after all?' she said doubtfully. 'That man is cunning enough to attempt heading us off somewhere near home.'

Because he had no satisfactory answer to his sister's question as to the possible route the gipsy might have taken after losing sight of them, but anxious to set Margaret's mind at ease, he said firmly: 'The fellow wouldn't dare trying to stop us reaching home. Father scared him too much that day when he caught him in the vegetable garden.'

Jimmie paused, staring across the valley pensively, sensing, rather than feeling, the security the strath offered.

'My guess is,' he went on, 'the fellow has probably given up the chase knowing it to be hopeless to continue. Besides, he'd have Hunter to deal with as well. Anyway, Maggie, he could be charged by the police if he tried to molest us.'

His last words were intended to convey to his sister that her fears were groundless; but he only partially succeeded in this respect, her fear and knowledge of the gipsy's bad reputation having taken on enormous proportions in her present nervous condition of mind.

'I only hope you're right,' came her doubtful reply. She was greatly concerned above all else at what the man might or might not do for the sake of the reward money. To her, as a travelling man, he was completely ruthless and inscrutable. Neither she nor Jimmie had given the reward money a second thought after their Aunt Ellen had mentioned it, repeating the sum constantly as if it were a sin to offer so much for a mere dog. Margaret knew she had been thinking of some of the poorer crofters' children who could be better fed on it.

As for themselves, they had been too shocked to think that Hunter was so highly valued by his master, followed by the stark realization that their last fragile hopes of trying to get their father to buy the dog for them had now truly gone. That they themselves might be entitled to it had never entered their heads. Even now, sitting there alone with Hunter in the valley, with the knowledge that the gipsy's sole object was to get the dog for himself, it still did not occur to either that they were now being regarded as possible rivals for the money. All they cared about was that they had Hunter safe, and were taking him home.

While they rested after their lunch, Hunter got up, going back slowly along the route they had taken on entering the valley. They watched him through half-closed eyes, knowing he was only bent on reconnoitring on his own to ensure their safety. Neither had any fear he was going to desert them, merely conscious that he was intent on protecting them from any sudden appearance of the gipsy.

Having no knowledge of what the alsatian had discovered at the raven's lake, and Hunter's hatred of the scent he found not only there but on the half-drowned collie, the gipsy would have fared badly had he entered the valley, not only out of Hunter's enmity for past cruelties, but in defence of the children themselves whom he cared so much about.

Jimmie and Margaret noticed the dog's gait was leisurely. There were moments when he stopped, testing the spurts of air that came from the west. They told him little, certainly nothing to rouse his suspicions. For the most part they were mere currents of air from around the western flank of Branstree ridge, being part of the varying flow from the north-east. Hunter's objective was the crags through which ran the track. If the gipsy was still in pursuit, it would be along the route the children had taken to reach this quiet, secluded place.

A sudden misgiving that perhaps Hunter was slowly making his way back to Harter Fell made Jimmie focus his field glasses on the dog. Just as that misgiving was about to become a fixation in his mind, Hunter turned and came loping back. He had satisfied himself that nobody was on that track leading from Branstree. Jimmie and Margaret were, for the time being at least, perfectly safe. Nevertheless, because of that evil taint he had found in the air-streams, Hunter was fully alerted for any emergency. He was conscious of the utmost caution to be adopted when they finally quitted the valley, no matter by what route. The instincts of the police-dog strain in him allowed for no complete relaxation, and for once he was not thinking so much of his master as he was of the children for whom he felt a special responsibility. He was ready to ensure that no harm befell them.

By the time he reached them, the rucksack had been re-packed and as Jimmie and Margaret stretched themselves out on the grass beside the tarn, enjoying the sun which, in the valley, poured down its golden glory of warmth, Hunter lay on all fours beside them, panting gently, but constantly keeping watch over them.

16

Remembering that they had promised to be home early to greet their parents on their arrival, the children, with Hunter, started off, moving northwards out of the sun-enclosed valley, leaving the only near habitation, Sadgill, away off in the south. As they climbed out of the strath, they were faced with the stiffening breeze from the north-east. After the heat in the valley, they were compelled to zip up their jackets, the breeze now coming at them in sharp, sudden gusts.

'It's quite cold after being in the valley so long,' Jimmie gasped as he was struck by what appeared to him to be a sustained revolving gust.

'The wind changes direction so often up here,' Margaret answered, lowering her head against it. 'I've noticed this happening before when we've been on Shap Fells.' As she spoke, with an upward glance at the sky, she saw small fleeces of cloud flying high above them. One thing she was sure of was that they held no threat of rain.

' "Mackerel sky, twelve hours dry",' Margaret said to herself more than to her brother. Jimmie, however, a step behind her caught the drift of her folklore quotation.

'Hence the gusty wind,' he shouted lest his words be carried away, but his sister heard him all right, for she nodded her head.

They were now at a point above the Ralfland Forest – a forest in name only, for it was mainly rough, hummocky moorland with an expanding area of scrub. Jimmie decided to spy out the surrounding landscape through his field glasses, the better to ascertain exactly where they were.

He observed, quite a distance away, the main road to Penrith, and after a further adjustment of the lens, could see the railway line running close beside it with what, he assumed, must be Shap summit signal box, hidden and with only the upper portion showing because of the snow fences on the embankment. Beyond it he thought he

could discern what could only be the scattered buildings of the granite works.

Jimmie shook his head meditatively. To head off across the fells in the direction of the road would take them a long time, with still a couple of miles more to go before reaching the left-hand turn to Bampton. In the long run, to have gone that way would have been distinctly to their advantage, and undoubtedly they would have escaped much that happened to them before evening.

As it was Jimmie abandoned without further thought any idea of making for the road and Shap summit, and concentrated on making a survey of the fells stretching in a series of corrugated folds directly ahead of him.

This entailed him altering his stance to retain a secure foothold on the uneven ground, bringing him a little more to the west and the afternoon sun. Again his fingers worked nimbly to readjust the lens in order to pick up some easily recognizable landmark between the ruins of Shap Abbey and the eastern approaches of the Swindale Beck as it issued from out of Gatescarth Pass. He was now more certain of their position in relationship to Rosgill, but his action brought a winking gleam to one who was watching carefully as he lay completely hidden in the scrubland on the outer edge of the forest. It came across the intervening space like a flashing of a beacon light. The man's beady eyes narrowed to bring into greater prominence the shapes of the children and the dog who accompanied them.

He gave a grunt of satisfaction, knowing his hunch had paid off.

With a wriggling motion, much impeded by the net on his back, he pressed himself closer into the scrub, hoping to avoid detection. All the while, he kept his gaze on the children and the dog as they started to move from fell to fell. Now was the time when he could well lose sight of them. The dales on Shap were deep and widely scattered, but he kept a mental image of where they might be and the direction they were bent on taking. When momentarily they vanished a little longer than usual, relief only came to him when they reappeared on another ridge, making him positive that they were keeping west of the beck that rose on the high moors above Bretherdale Head. Yet he had many moments of misgiving, for so often were they out of sight in some valley that it was only by constant watching that finally he was able to make a random guess as to their ultimate destination where a dash for Rosgill would become possible.

The gipsy felt a growing impatience as he watched, impotently, while they toiled from ridge to ridge, but he was sure they were bent on reaching the narrow road from Keld as soon as they reached less hilly ground. Although this idea persisted in his mind, he yet had an impression that they were, at no time, getting nearer to where he lay, waiting. He could not understand it at all.

Possessing nothing in the way of imagination, the phenomenon was deeply puzzling. There must, he argued within himself, be some reason for it, ignoring what to any other would have been a simple explanation. The terrain was so exactly similar wherever one looked, that distance and movement were utterly deceptive and out of proportion in relationship to the nearest ridge or summit height.

The gipsy was fairly trembling with frustration and impatience.

After keeping them in view for well over half an hour, and seeming still farther than ever from Ralfland Forest, one possible solution came to him as something of a shock. They were following as best they could the winding course of the beck which ran east, and not west. The gipsy then recalled with intense fury that there was a footpath from Shap Abbey that would take them straight to Rosgill and not to Bampton.

'It's that scheming boy,' he muttered angrily. 'He knows the way he should go all right. Just like a kid . . .' he trailed off scornfully.

In actual fact, Jimmy was not altogether confident of the route he was so doggedly following. All he knew with any certainty was that the main road was on his right, hidden by the hills. One thing he was sure about was that the beck they followed could only be the one that passed close to Ralfland Forest at one point, and then on to Keld.

Saying nothing to his sister so as not to alarm her, he was exceedingly angry with himself for not having brought his map with him. It must have been the first time he had forgotten, he thought sullenly, due, he supposed, to their leaving home so hurriedly that morning. Now he would have to rely entirely on that sense of direction he so often boasted he possessed, but being out of sight of the Cumbrian Mountains, with each ridge and fell surrounding them appearing so much alike, he would have to continue on, hoping in the end to reach Keld and Shap Abbey.

Finally the sense of being lost proved too much for him to resist further. 'I'll soon take another bearing through the glasses,' he said to his sister with exaggerated nonchalance.

Margaret was not in the least deceived by his assumed indifference. For the past ten minutes or more she had the conviction that all was not going as well as it should. More and more she was depending on Hunter to see them through, protect them should it be necessary, although she did manage to say with a smile: 'We'll have to climb that ridge first before you can use your glasses to any effect.'

'I know!' was the grim retort.

Hunter was hard at Margaret's heels, time and time again, testing the wind currents that came off the fells. He also had the feeling they were off course . . . especially for Harter Fell where he had expected them to go.

The beck at this point, following the contour of the dale and the pebbly bed it had made for itself over many years, swept around in a loop to the east, with the outskirts of Ralfland Forest not too far away in the west.

They were, in fact, much nearer than the gipsy thought – only a whale-backed ridge hiding them.

Just when it seemed they could be very near indeed,

the ridge turned due east, going away from the forest as the northern edge sloped down again to the beck and Keld. The gipsy seeing them in silhouette, and apparently so close, was now beside himself with glee. 'Now I'll have them . . . frighten them off and get the dog entangled in the net. Now . . . Now!' He was about to go into action, sure of ultimate success, when the bile of hatred that had been with him all day welled up in his heart and he threw away any further desire for caution. He ran shouting along the scrubland, with the net slipping half-way down his back, causing him to stumble again and again.

Until then, Jimmie, with his careful survey of the outlying landscape, had not focused on the immediate foreground where the gipsy had concealed himself so well. The sudden shouting and the surprising emergence of the man from the scrub below, whilst giving the children a swift penetration of fear, did not quite bring about the same reaction they had experienced on the summit pass of Branstree. Then it was alarm for Hunter who had left them, thinking he had found his master. Now the situation was different. It was as though they had, in their hearts, expected something of the kind to happen, whilst refusing to acknowledge it to themselves and so discuss what they should do in the circumstances that now squarely confronted them.

Jimmie realized at once the gipsy's intent, as did Margaret, and to a lesser degree, Hunter himself. The alsatian, however, had no fears. He knew what he would have to do if the children were threatened. Jimmie was more sure of himself by now, knowing their exact position on the fells.

'Take no notice,' he commanded authoritatively. 'We'll pretend we've not seen him and proceed straight along the ridge and just hope we can make Keld.' Seeing Margaret's hand instinctively gripping the dog's collar, he pulled a length of cord from his pocket, instructing his sister to tie it for a leash. 'That'll keep him close to us . . . just in case. . . .'

Although Jimmie had through his field glasses seen both the Swindale Beck and Hawes Water, together with the road to Bampton, he knew that with the gipsy below and so near they could not now make across country to Mardale Common and Rosgill which he had also glimpsed so clearly.

Surprised as he was that they were so near their destination and now so helpless in reaching it, he was striving hard to think up a plan to outwit the gipsy. He turned his gaze along the whole ridge in the direction of Keld and Shap Abbey. There was one ploy left to them now – that of complete boldness in the face of possible danger.

Margaret, who had not uttered a word all this time, proceeded to follow her brother's advice, Hunter looking up at her in surprise. This was the first time they had ever restricted his movements, and he was not only perplexed, but more widely alerted to the actuality of impending threat. However, he submitted good-naturedly to the tethering, knowing that in the event of action he could easily slip his head through the chain collar that hung loosely about his neck. They then proceeded along the ridge, moving slowly and facing the constantly gusting wind.

Hunter never let the leaping shape below them out of sight, and there were moments when Margaret had difficulty in keeping him strictly under control. At last she held him closer to her, holding him by the collar itself while looping the cord around her arm. She saw Hunter's muzzle wrinkle in a snarl, and heard the deep growl that kept rising in his throat.

'I'm sure Hunter would kill him if he touched us,' Jimmie said grimly. 'We've just to make it off the ridge and then see that the fellow doesn't move in too close.'

'He has a net or something with him,' Margaret answered. 'I am positive he intends trapping Hunter in it.'

'We'll soon see about that,' her brother replied tersely, as they all reached the steep slope down to the beck. From the survey he had made with his field glasses, he felt that Keld could not be more than three miles away across the fells, but he admitted to himself that it would be stiff going. Whatever else they might do to outstrip the gipsy, one thing was certain. They must keep on the move and not give up or panic.

The gipsy had kept them in sight until they left the ridge, wondering why they had put the dog on a tether. The thought that perhaps they intended setting the animal loose to attack him roused a simmering violence in him. 'I'll soon put paid to their little game,' he almost screamed, patting the net, now beside himself with rage as he thrust his way out of the thigh-high scrub and on to the open moorland thick with gorse and wind-twisted bushes.

His rage at the possibility of being thwarted had reached a state of near madness. Making another wild guess at the likely direction the children and the dog were going, he stumbled and fought his way over the rough ground. 'It's down by the beck I'll surely get them,' he kept saying, pushing himself forward at a rate that was taking its toll on his energies. His fury was such that he never realized when he had reached, and actually passed, the point of likely exhaustion. He did not know that his legs were stumbling over the uneven ground, and that the gorse bushes were plucking at and tearing his clothes, making them worse than ever.

Saliva trickled from his lips on to his chin, only to be wiped away by a brush of his arm and an inarticulate curse. He was already seeing himself beaten even now . . . beaten by two kids whom he knew were terrified of him . . . Or were they? he asked himself. Weren't they just a little too sure of themselves, relying on the dog to help them should the need arise? To and fro went his tormented thoughts, his breath becoming a gasping wheeze as his heart throbbed painfully in his chest. He managed a grotesque laugh at the thought of the alsatian free of the temporary leash and making a leap at him . . . straight into the outspread net. He had no doubt he could be a tough beast to enmesh and hold securely in a net made by his wife for the lifting of salmon from the Solway Firth on an ebb tide.

Still, no matter the cost in physical discomfort to himself, he'd do it to get even with the Thornton kids and put that fifty pounds' reward money in his pocket. It would all come out right in the end. Breathless and weary though he was, he had no doubts about it.

Although he was not aware of the fact, he had actually outpaced the children when in what he thought was a last desperate effort he waded across the beck a quarter of a mile ahead of them. Here the heath was more densely covered with flowering gorse and newly born heather.

A burst of coughing brought him to a stumbling halt, breathless and choking and beside himself with uncontrollable anger. He stooped forward to ease his chest and in an attempt to regain his diminished strength. They have to come this way, he was thinking, or would they have made for the road?

He was no longer sure of himself, thinking that maybe after all, that fifty pounds were irretrievably lost to him . . . Fifty pounds!

Then in a spate of temper, edging on to complete irresponsibility, he searched in his pockets for a box of matches. He'd stop them! He'd do it by firing the gorse and so cutting off their last remaining escape route. . . .

Regardless of the constantly varying direction of the wind, he quickly had a sheet of flame springing up before him . . . flame which crackled and made the gorse cry out in agony as bush after bush was swept by blasting heat and smoke rose over the fells. A flying spark held in the northerly air-flow caught the bushes the other side of the beck, and soon both sides of the water course were ringed about with fire.

17

It was late in the afternoon when John and Mary Thornton drove slowly through Bampton and took the secondary road to Rosgill. Thornton himself, concentrating on the road ahead, did not look out across the fells as did his wife. She suddenly exclaimed that there was a heath fire raging over on Shap Fells. 'It seems bad from here,' she said, her brow puckered as she stared out across the slow unwinding of the Swindale Beck and Shap Abbey.

Her husband drew the car to a halt at the side of the road. His face, lean and brown, but quite unwrinkled, with hair slightly greying at the sides, turned so that his mild blue eyes followed the direction she had indicated.

'It certainly does appear to be a bad outbreak, and sweeping around in a circle due to the wind, no doubt. I wonder what caused it?' he concluded thoughtfully.

'Perhaps a burning cinder from one of the train engines,' his wife replied.

Thornton shook his head emphatically. 'The centre of the fire is too far from the railway,' he answered, 'and there's no farm near that could be clearing ground for future planting.'

At that precise moment a cyclist appeared, pedalling rapidly with his head well down. His thin legs, encased in trousers gripped tightly by clips at the ankles, gave him the local name by which he was generally known – Police Sergeant 'Leggy'. He pulled up with a jerk beside the car, panting after so much exertion. 'Hoping to break a record in getting to Bampton?' John Thornton asked in good humour.

The constable – for that was what he really was,

although everybody in Bampton referred to him as Sergeant — greeted both John and Mary Thornton enthusiastically before saying: 'That fire is goin' to get out of control in this rising wind. Wonder what set it a-goin' like that?' He seemed to be pondering the question in his mind.

'We're just wondering that same thing,' John Thornton answered. 'Perhaps when you get to Bampton you had better get some beaters out.'

'I was thinking that myself as I was coming along.' Then as if a thought had suddenly struck him, 'Wonder if some fool is trying to flush out that missing dog all the fuss is about?'

'What dog?' husband and wife asked together.

The constable explained, stating a big reward was offered for his recovery. His owner had recently gone to Langholm to bring back another of his type. . . . 'Expert in trackin',' he said in doubtful tones, 'like those police dogs we hear so much about, but never get. The fellow should be back at the hotel in Patterdale by now. I understand he was returning today, determined to find that missing dog of his.'

Mary Thornton turned to her husband. 'That man with the estate car which he parked alongside us at Carlisle, he had a big dog with him.'

'Could it have been one of them alsatians, ma'am?' the constable asked before her husband could reply.

'It certainly was,' she replied. 'Don't you remember, John?' she asked.

'I do indeed. He was one of the largest of the breed I have ever seen. I remember too the way he vanished, his master with him. The waiter said the man was anxious to get away, and both had gone before we got down to breakfast.'

'That's the feller, sure enough,' the constable answered quickly. 'Do you remember what he looked like?'

Both shook their heads, John Thornton merely remarking on the size and obvious good breeding of the dog.

'That'll be the feller all right. He breeds them sort of dogs as a kind of hobby. Wins prizes with them, I believe.' Up to that point in their conversation his tones were merely of an enquiring nature. Suddenly, as if recalling his position as the keeper of law and order in the locality, he adopted a very official voice when he said abruptly: 'I'd better be off right away then, and ring the hotel as soon as I get to the station,' which remark caused the Thorntons to smile, regarding the police station as a cottage in which the constable lived, expressing his authority by the notice board outside the building. 'I'll get some beaters out on the fells too,' he shouted back over his shoulder as he cycled away, his thin legs moving in perfect rhythm from long experience.

John Thornton also drove on towards Rosgill, Mary watching the distant spread of fire with deepening apprehension. 'There's an awful lot of smoke with the flames,' she said once, 'and the wind is causing the flames to cover a wider area....'

Her apprehension turned to speechless dismay and shock as they drove up to the house to be greeted by Ellen, standing in the porch, white-faced and near to distraction. 'The children ...' she gasped out, without a word of greeting. 'They're missing.... Been out all day since early morning.... Promised to be back early....'

John Thornton switched off the ignition and jumped out of the car. Her broken utterances told of her great distress, and taking her gently by the arm, he led her into the house. His wife shakingly followed, forgetting their luggage and her parcels.

'Now calm yourself, Ellen,' John Thornton was saying quietly. 'It's not all that late.'

'They said they'd be home early so as to be here when you arrived, and there's that fierce alsatian loose on the fells. I was surprised they were going out today and I should have guessed they had something in mind when I saw Jimmie with that big rucksack on his back just as they struck off from the house towards the pass.... I wouldn't have seen them at all but for my standing at the large window on the landing looking out across the fells. If they've come across that dog!' Her voice faltered and fear was in her wide-open eyes. 'He'd be starving and fierce, as he's been loose for days now.... I only heard about him yesterday...' she ended lamely, appearing absolutely helpless in what she regarded as a situation she could not cope with.

John Thornton was thinking. 'That dog again! The constable mentioned him in connection with that heath fire on Shap. I wonder if he was right ... and somebody is trying to flush him out and if the children are with him?'

For an instant he felt himself to be as helpless as the woman before him.

Turning abruptly to his wife, he said gently: 'Don't worry, Mary.... Nor you, Ellen. The kids will be all right. They're well able to take care of themselves.' Then speaking directly to Aunt Ellen, he referred to the rucksack. 'I'll go to the outhouse and see which of them Jimmie has taken. There are two.'

He returned a few minutes later, his face set and serious. During his absence Ellen had made a pot of strong tea, and she and Mary were sitting at the table. John Thornton joined them.

Mary looked up in nervous anticipation of what her husband had to say as he sipped thoughtfully – very thoughtfully, she felt – the cup of tea that had been handed to him.

He spoke to Ellen first. 'That missing dog?' he queried. 'How long has he been presumed lost?'

'Nearly a week, from what I heard,' she answered.

'What has the dog to do with the children being late

in returning home, John?' Mary inquired anxiously. 'You don't think they found him and he savaged them?'

'Hardly that,' he replied, somewhat drily.

'Then what do you think?'

'I'm not altogether sure of what to think . . . yet! One thing *you* can be sure about is that if they should by chance have come across him, he'd hardly harm them.' He spoke with utmost confidence on this – the most vital point his wife worried about.

Before she could question him further, he ascertained from Ellen that the children had been out on the fells every day, taking their meals with them. 'I was surprised this morning to find them up early, ready to go out,' she finally remarked regretfully. 'I thought they'd want to stop home as they were so excited when you phoned. Margaret has said more than once that she'd be glad when you got back home.'

John nodded his head thoughtfully, his mind now concentrating on another, different, avenue of conjecture.

'I hope they did not think me too severe because I'm what they would term "a school marm". I let them do as they wished, within limits of course.'

'I'm absolutely positive you've done what we, their parents, would have done. They like being out of doors. It's Jimmie taking that rucksack that puzzles me. Did he take it every day?'

'Not to my knowledge,' the children's Aunt Ellen confessed at once. 'I wouldn't have known this morning but for my going to the landing window and seeing them making for the track up to the pass.'

'What is exactly worrying you, John?' his wife asked, alarm showing in her eyes.

He turned and rested his hand tenderly on her shoulder, telling her not to worry. 'Everything is quite all right as far as I can foresee.' He went on to relate what he had discovered and the possible reason why they had taken the rucksack they usually carried on all-day expeditions on the fells. It was with a hint of laughter in his eyes that he added that it wasn't all they had taken.

'They've nearly stripped the outside larder,' he said. 'That carcass of lamb is little more than a skeleton, and Mary, love, they've taken most of the good tinned foods you've been storing up.'

'But they had their own haversacks with them, and I cut fresh sandwiches every day,' Aunt Ellen interjected with a flushed face.

'I've not the slightest doubt you did them very well indeed; but I think they were feeding something, or somebody else who couldn't fend for himself.'

'The dog!' Mary exclaimed suddenly. 'They had found that alsatian.'

Her husband agreed, stating that in his opinion the animal had been injured and Jimmie and Margaret had hidden him away until they could bring him home. 'Now,' he said slowly, 'they can't because they're cut off by that fire we saw on Shap Fells. You dish up dinner, Ellen,' John then added, 'while I telephone the constable at Bampton, and get that fellow's hotel and number at Patterdale . . . the chap that owns the dog,' he concluded briefly, hurrying into the hallway to make the call.

He was absent for some minutes, during which, to occupy her mind, Mary helped Ellen to set out the dinner. Not for a moment did she consider Jimmie and Margaret to be under any threat other than, perhaps, from that of the heath fire. She was sure now that her husband had been right, and thinking of the missing stores in the outside larder, she found herself wondering what the dog would look like. 'Over-fed, no doubt,' she decided, 'but docile. . . .'

When her husband rejoined them at the table he expressed satisfaction at the meal placed before him. Noticing his wife and Aunt Ellen looking at him in what was nothing short of an unuttered inquiry, anxiously awaited, he explained that he and the police had been on to the dog's owner whose name was Duncan Walsh. 'It was the man whose estate car was parked alongside ours at Carlisle,' he said, looking directly at his wife. 'He's coming over right away, bringing his dog with him.'

'It's getting so late,' Mary Thornton said, panic in her voice as she thought of the children.

'They'll be quite all right,' John answered with much the same assurance as displayed by his son. 'It's my guess they've been cut off by that fire, and have been forced to make an extra long trek to get home. . . . That's all! I bet, anyway, they'll have that dog with them, looking fine after the food they've fed him with. Best carcass of lamb that was,' he concluded, smiling openly.

For some reason or other, possibly due to the reassuring tone he had adopted, the two women smiled also, Mary thinking that he clearly was of the same opinion as herself, only she decided the animal would surely appear grossly over-fed.

'Best keep some of this excellent food for our guest as he was not waiting for dinner at the hotel. He'll probably have to stay for the night, and there might be just enough pickings on that carcass outside for that huge alsatian he's bringing along.'

As soon as she had finished her meal, Ellen hurried away to prepare the guest room for their expected new arrival, Duncan Walsh, asking as she departed: 'Where will we put the dog?'

John shook his head, shrugging his shoulders at the same time. 'Best let's see him first at close quarters and then let his master decide.'

He and his wife then rose from the table, going into the front living room where a log fire blazed on the hearth, and sat down to await the Scotsman's appearance. It was the same room which, only a few evenings before, had loomed largely in the children's imagination as they hastened home after spending their first day with Hunter. Mary could not sit still. She constantly went over to the window, peering out over the fells and dales upon which the darkness seemed to be settling quickly that night, while in the east an orange glow rose and fell where the heath fire still burned in the direction of Shap.

Although he was not allowing any sign of distress to show on his face, John Thornton was now admitting to be extremely worried, hoping strongly that his suggestion the children were being delayed by the heath fire was, in fact, right, and that nothing worse had befallen them. One thing he was confident about, they would be perfectly safe if indeed they had the dog with them. Of that there could be little doubt. They were not handling a half-starved animal, judging from what remained of the lamb carcass in the outer larder. 'The cheek of them,' he muttered, trying to conjure up the scene of one or other of the children stealing out, possibly under Ellen's very nose, to carve up the carcass to feed a lost dog. 'I bet it was young Jimmie, and that dog, if he's not too badly hurt, has been having the time of his life with the two kids looking after him and attending to his injuries. . . .'

In contrast to her husband's apparent calm, Mary Thornton could not conceal her growing anxiety, and was on the point of suggesting that they phone the police again, this time to get a search party out for the children. She had momentarily forgotten the dog in her acute mental distress, and, as the dusk deepened into almost complete darkness, the sullen glow on Shap Fells seemed more menacing than ever – a dancing, leaping flame of light.

Mary's thoughts as she continued to watch that dancing glow on the horizon were broken suddenly by the bright headlights of a car that swung off the road into the drive, announcing the arrival of Duncan Walsh. Her husband hurried to the door to welcome him, and she heard a soft Scots voice bidding him 'Good evening'.

The next moment she was being introduced to a tallish man in well-tailored tweeds with the beautiful German shepherd dog she had seen in the estate car at Carlisle. On command from his master, the animal sat quietly at his heels, seeming entirely at ease in a strange house.

18

Hunter was the first to become conscious of the new threat ahead. His widely spread nostrils caught the pungent smell of smoke before it drifted into the dale by way of the beck, or showed itself above the skyline. In a very determined effort to warn Margaret of the danger, he pulled back on the grip she had on his collar, and sitting on his hunkers, whined and looked up into her face. His look was wistful, almost as if in apology for his attitude. 'What is it, Hunter?' she asked. Her brother had stopped also, the awareness of something unusual awakened by the dog's refusal to proceed further.

'He senses something is wrong . . . something we know nothing about,' he said suddenly. 'You stay here with him, Margaret. I'll crawl up that hump ahead and have a look through my glasses. Don't worry. Hunter will look after you.'

'What if it's that gipsy?' she whispered. 'He's crazy enough to harm you.'

'We'll see!' Jimmie replied grimly, moving off and creeping up the hummock around which the beck looped through widening banks, fringed with reeds. Margaret saw her brother stop short of the top and bring out his field glasses. She had the instant impression that he had already seen what Hunter had sensed. He stayed prone for some seconds, taking in every aspect of the scene below him. Then putting his glasses back into his haversack, he started to stumble back to where she stood, waiting with bated breath.

Before he reached her, she saw it – a whirling wisp of smoke being blown along the course of the beck. It came in sinuous whorls at first, then clinging to the top of the water as if held by the dampness.

'What is it?' she asked breathlessly, as her brother hastened up, angry and eyes blazing with a rage he could scarcely restrain.

'That gipsy!' he announced with dramatic intensity. 'He's set fire to the scrub, and it's blazing on both sides of the beck, fanned by the wind, I suppose. Sparks are flying all over the place.' Then, with the first note of helplessness she had heard in his voice all that day in spite of their many trials and anxieties, he said: 'It seems he's cut us off from Shap Abbey and the road. He's down there waiting, and it appears to me he's overcome with glee, or just plain mad. He certainly thinks he's got us well and truly trapped.'

'Can't we possibly escape?' Margaret asked, with tears in her voice.

'We're going to have a jolly good try.' By now the smoke was thickening in the dale, and rising high above the hummock Jimmie had climbed. Then in an upward rush they saw the first lick of flame on a solitary clump of heather that crowned it; the next moment, the heather was just another furiously blazing bush. They could hear its crackling agony from where they stood.

'Let's move back a bit,' Jimmie said, 'following each dale as we come to it. That gippo is expecting us to make a break for it by way of the beck, but he's going to have a long wait. One thing's he's overlooked is that such a blaze is going to attract somebody's attention, but we shan't be able to make for home that way. . . .'

The sun was westering fast, and already it was gloomy in the dales. Jimmie was thinking with calculated calmness now, trying to seek another solution to the problem of getting back to Rosgill. He had already realized it couldn't possibly be done until well after nightfall. Moreover, the fells were dangerous to traverse in the dark. There were so many steep slopes, strewn with boulders. This aspect of restricted movement troubled him more than any other.

'Mother and Father will be home by now, and angry at our being away,' his sister murmured tearfully. 'If it gets very late, they'll be terribly worried.'

Jimmie, who had been expecting such a remark from Margaret, was prompt in his reply. 'They'll possibly telephone the police and get up a search party.' Jimmie spoke with the return of his old confidence.

'But to put them to all that anxiety and trouble after such a long journey from the North of Scotland,' faltered Margaret. 'Oh, Jimmie! What can we do?'

Her brother slid his arm around her again to comfort her as he answered quickly enough: 'We'll have to make our way back to the hidden valley and tarn. We can make it before dark, and the gipsy won't be anywhere near to threaten us.'

This was the plan he secretly built up in his mind, keeping it to himself in order not to distress Margaret further. What he withheld was the notion that if the worst happened, and they could not proceed in the dark, they would have to spend the night in the valley. They could then make their way home by way of Branstree and the Gatescarth Pass as soon as it was light. He did not expect any further trouble from the gipsy. The fellow would wait beyond the boundary of the fire he had made, presuming they would make their attempt to break through to Keld in the dusk. 'He'll be disappointed,' Jimmie said with obvious satisfaction.

'Who?' Margaret asked, her thoughts elsewhere.

'That gipsy fellow, of course. He'll keep on waiting for us to make a dash for it along the beck to avoid the hot ground. It's quite shallow there. Won't he be disappointed, though?'

Jimmie strode on ahead as quickly as he could, with

Hunter, now released from the restriction of the cord, running freely. He kept close to the rear, alert to any sound that presaged danger, but feeling less apprehensive, hoping they were now on the way back to Harter Fell.

There was a short-lived sepia-tinted glow over the western edge of the dale they followed, and the children knew then that the sun had gone down behind the Cumbrian Mountains. Soon the dusk would be turning into complete darkness, and they had to reach the valley before then.

Margaret was not only very troubled, but was finding it hard to hold back her tears. The near approach of darkness, and they all alone on the fells save for Hunter in whom they must now have complete trust, was something that in her suppressed state of terror made her imagine events that would never before have occurred to her. Her comfort, such as it was, lay not so much in Jimmie, but in Hunter.

Her brother was forging ahead with a marked determination to achieve his objective. Often he stumbled badly where, in the gloom, his feet encountered broken ground. They went from dale to dale, following the winding course of the beck which sounded loud in the night hush. 'Ah, we've reached the shallows,' Jimmie muttered. 'Now for the long climb up the fell. . . .' He stopped, waiting for his sister and Hunter to catch up with him. For the first time since they were very small children, he put both arms around her, hugging her and murmuring: 'Sorry I've been hurrying on so quickly. You mustn't be frightened. By now Mother and Father will know we've somehow got lost on the fells, and undoubtedly have already arranged for a search party to look for us. They'll probably think we've been cut off by that fire. . . .'

There was but a brief moment of embarrassment between them, and this Margaret herself dispelled by a fleeting smile at her brother.

'It's quite all right,' she replied. 'You see, Hunter was always close behind me in case. . . .'

It was an instinctive action on the part of both to glance back, Margaret aware of being deeply moved by Jimmie's unexpected display of concern for her. The sight that met their eyes was incredible, and made them gasp. All along that northern skyline was a shuddering vehemence of colour and flying sparks carried on the wind. Smoke, driven by that same wind, assumed a curious luminescence as it sped like a darkening cloud over the fells.

'That chap's set something going that'll not be easily put out,' Jimmie said on bated breath. 'The ground is so dry just now. He's done for himself now, sure enough.'

'I hope so,' was Margaret's reply, her mind already leaping ahead to the stark realization that it was only they who knew he had caused it. She hoped with all her heart that Jimmie was right, and that he was crazy enough to stay on Shap Fells waiting for them to try and get home that way despite the fire. 'Then we'll certainly be safe,' she whispered, ensuring that Jimmie did not hear.

Her brother, however, was busy in bringing Hunter to the fore, ordering him to lead the way. The dog looked up at him enquiringly, as if not quite understanding what was required of him. Then, pointing to the ground, Jimmie uttered the word he did know: 'Seek!' Whilst not knowing what he was expected to seek, Hunter was shrewd enough to perceive that the children were anxious to go back, perhaps to Harter Fell.

With his nose to the ground, and his tail raised to the level of his back, he led them over the intervening dales and fells that separated them from the valley. Each time they went along one or other of the narrow dales they could hear the chattering voice of the beck, and because they were now becoming accustomed to the deepening dusk, Jimmie knew that Hunter led the way with unerring certainty, and that soon they would be at the northern ridge hiding the valley.

Thinking of the map Jimmie had forgotten to bring, Margaret asked timidly: 'You didn't forget your torch also?'

'No! That's always in my haversack, but I daren't use it here . . . just in case. . . .'

'You said the gipsy was on the opposite side of the fire he had started.'

'So he was, but nobody can guess what that fellow might get up to. He might even attempt wading up the beck, but that seems very unlikely from the way he was acting. He fully expected us to make a dash for it down the beck. He couldn't do anything now. The fire had too great a hold. I'll use the torch when we reach the tarn and try to find a place to rest in.'

'Jimmie! We must get home . . . we must!' Margaret cried out wildly.

Her brother once again put his arm around her now shaking shoulders. 'Do try trusting me, Maggie,' he implored. 'Everything will turn out for the best. Father will have a search party out for us by now, and it could be dangerous in the dark making for Gatescarth Pass. We could run into that gipsy fellow making his way to his camping site near Kilnshaw Chimney. We can rest up for a bit and be away again at daybreak. . . . Besides, it's still a long way to Rosgill from the valley.'

Margaret knew her brother was right, and putting complete trust in him and Hunter, steeled herself against the ordeal of having to sleep out that night.

Soon afterwards they came off the heights and down into the quietness and warmth of the valley. After the bleakness of the wind behind them it was like a garment wrapping itself around them, embracing them and giving cheer to their flagging spirits. Without hesitation, the children felt safe as if they had actually reached home.

Although it was now utterly dark and the stars bright overhead, the valley itself appeared to have retained a little of the heat the sun had brought to it during the day, and it was comforting.

They reached the tarn, now a starlit mirror with the uprising cliffs like an immense wall cutting off all access to the outside world. Jimmie was now able to use his torch, partially concealing the beam with the palm of his hand. He found an overhang with moss at its foot, and some closely cropped grass. This indication that rabbits used the spot gave him the assurance that it was a safe and unvisited place.

'We'll bunk down here with our haversacks for pillows, but we'll have something to eat first . . . our supper in, fact,' he said with a grin which his sister guessed was on his face, but could not see.

As he doled out more of the food, and drained the last of the lemonade into the plastic glasses, the thought crossed his mind as to what had prompted him to bring more food than usual, particularly so much meat for Hunter. Had he an obscure feeling that something would go wrong that day? Was there really substance in the notion of premonition?

Margaret at last said she was tired, and Jimmie made her as comfortable as possible, peeling off his anorak to put over her to keep her warm. Jimmie took up a position beside her, while Hunter stretched out alongside him, the heat from his body giving the boy a measure of comfort.

Once an owl hooted, causing Margaret to stir restlessly, but Jimmie's arm about her lulled her back into semi-sleep.

Meanwhile, Hunter remained stretched closely against the boy, his ears alert, and never at any time utterly relaxed. He knew he had to keep them safe through the hours of darkness. . . .

19

John and Mary Thornton, and Aunt Ellen also, took an immediate liking to Duncan Walsh, and certainly an unconcealed admiration for the beautiful alsatian who sat so quietly beside him. Walsh, anxious to get down to the tracking of the children and undoubtedly his dog Hunter, admitted to being hungry, saying they could make plans while he ate the splendid supper Ellen set before him. Before he could check her she had also given Max a dish of meat, Duncan shaking his head in disapproval, saying the animal should not have been fed when he had work to do. 'It's so very little for an animal of his size,' she retorted with a smile. Walsh could not help smiling in return, remarking she had been very considerate.

Meanwhile, Duncan Walsh suggested they took along some sandwiches and a flask of coffee. 'It may take us all night,' he said, perusing the large-scale map set out before him, while his companion whispered something in Ellen's ear, and she nodded. Then as Mary Thornton could no longer keep back the tears that flooded her eyes, Duncan Walsh said, with infinite kindness in his voice, 'I'm positive it is going to be all right. Max here is one of the best trackers of his breed, and he'll find the children, and Hunter also, for I'm sure he's with them. That fire on the fells has forced the children to take another and possibly more difficult route home.'

After hearing more about the children's activities during the week, he inclined to the view that Hunter had been hurt in some way or another, and until he could get about without distress they had kept him in hiding, taking the food he required from the outside pantry. Said he, striving to be jocular in circumstances tense with anxiety, 'I'll have to put him on a diet when we get back to Langholm. . . . Almost half a lamb carcass, you say. . . .' He gave a low whistle.

The one remaining rucksack was got ready with sandwiches and a flask of hot coffee. Another smaller package was given to John Thornton, which he thrust hastily into his pocket as Walsh hurried outside to the car for his raincoat, saying as he returned and hustled himself into it: 'Just in case. . . .'

He then stood before them, a man of slimmish build, approaching middle age, with a face strong with the character he so obviously possessed – the character of a man who organized his life to a strict discipline, and yet allowed in it sufficient time for relaxation and enjoyment. His fingers were finely shaped and thin, and John Thornton could imagine them being extremely gentle when helping to bring puppies into the world.

Mary Thornton had the utmost confidence in him, as did her husband who recognized in the other a man similar in some ways to himself, but with widely differing aims in life.

All this time, Max sat waiting patiently. He knew he was required for something very special that night, and when his master asked for some garment of the children's to sniff, his tracking instincts were instantly aroused.

Duncan Walsh nodded, letting the alsatian sniff thoroughly one of Jimmie's recently discarded shirts and one of Margaret's blouses. Then thrusting them into each of his raincoat pockets, he said: 'We'll now let Max take over . . . completely. . . .' He attached a very long leash to the dog's collar, uttering just one word: 'Seek!'

Max set off without the slightest hesitation in manner, the two women standing in the porch watching the men and dog move rapidly down the drive, the alsatian loping along with the easy gait of his kind.

The women watched in silence, staring up the fell where they knew the track to be. Then a beam of light from a torch shattered the darkness, remaining steady for a moment, then moving farther and farther away as the men led by the dog followed the exact trail taken by Jimmie and Margaret earlier in the day. For a dog like Max, with the scent still reasonably fresh, he never once faltered, but kept forging steadily ahead.

In half an hour or so they had reached the green meadow common of Mardale with a dark smudge of fir-woods strumming a harmony of sibilant music in the still gusting wind from the north-east. A night bird passed in winnowing flight over their heads, but the dog did not deviate for one moment from the trail he followed, although he was aware of the owl flying past.

'Now for the most trying part,' John gasped, 'the ascent up the fells to Harter.'

'Harter?' queried Duncan Walsh.

'Yes. . . . It's one of the craggy heights hereabouts . . . over two thousand feet, I understand.'

'Craggy, you say? Has it cliffs with caves in it, do you know?'

'It's pretty well fissured in places,' John answered. 'I doubt if we'll find them there. It's well away from that fire on Shap, and there's nothing to stop them coming down off the fells for home.'

The other man was silent, thinking that perhaps they couldn't come because Hunter had met with further injury and could not walk. In such an event, he considered one or other of the children would have returned home for their father's advice and assistance. He decided that maybe they had been to this Harter place, and knowing this was likely to be their last day alone with the dog, had taken a different, longer route, to Rosgill, and indeed, as obviously John Thornton supposed, had been cut off by that fire on Shap Fells. He glanced over to the east.

There was still a smouldering glow on the horizon, indicating that the fire must have been very widespread. 'Wonder what caused it?' he asked himself, and while Max plodded steadily on, his nose to the scent he followed, Duncan Walsh allowed his mind to conjecture on the many possibilities that blaze opened up.

A bizarre effect was created by the torchlight. Grotesque shadows were cast against the slopes of the dale they had now reached, leading direct to the mouth of the pass. The beam moved up and down as the men pursued their silent, uphill way, the sound of the Swindale Beck coming up to them out of the darkness in a cacophony of sharps and trebles out of unison one with the other.

Thornton was full of admiration at Walsh's grit and determination in tackling the fellside without as much as a stop, concluding that Max was probably hauling him along. Actually, he was quite wrong. In the past, Duncan Walsh and Hunter together had often done more than a twenty-mile stint in the remote Highlands of Scotland, to which this was nothing out of the ordinary. Duncan knew from that past experience that once you had set a pace and got a flexibility of movement in the limbs, walking became easier as the lungs expanded to take the strain to breathe in more air. They had reached the worn footpath leading direct to Harter Fell before Duncan called a halt.

Max immediately came to heel, sitting beside his master, who, John perceived, was merely panting a little after the tremendous exertion he had made to reach this far. Thornton himself felt all in, breathing heavily and heartily glad of the respite.

'You've let yourself get out of condition,' was the only consolation he got. 'Anyway, we'll take a wee bit rest.'

They sat down on the rising edge of the track, John explaining that Harter was little more than a mile distant.

'That's where we'll find them,' Duncan answered with deep conviction.

John Thornton had his doubts, knowing that at least one of the children would have come home if the missing dog was still unable to walk for some reason or other. Behind him, the glow on Shap Fells was dying down, save for a sudden flicker of a blaze where yet another bush had been turned into a blazing torch by a flying spark, or the insidious creeping of fire under the surface of the heath – a not unusual event in the fell country.

It was near to midnight when, led by the indomitable Max, they saw in the darkness the awesome crags of Harter Fell looming up ahead, blacker even than the night itself against the bright stars above it.

Thornton called his children by name, softly. The whole place was haunted by an unearthly silence, disturbed only by an occasional whining of that north-easterly blow through its crags.

The beam from the torch shone unwaveringly on the seamed cliffs, while Max set industriously to work. He sniffed all around the base of the fell, picking up confusing sets of smells. Then he gave an excited whine, for he had picked up amongst the scents he had been following since leaving Rosgill that of his half-brother, Hunter. He immediately found the cleft, dragging Duncan forward in a sudden lunge. The torchlight hovered about the cleft, and Walsh, following Max, entered the cave.

'Come on in,' he shouted to John. 'They've been here all right. See for yourself!'

Thornton succeeded in creeping through the narrow entrance into the cave itself. The light from the torch moved from place to place. Everything was gradually revealed, the pan of fresh water set in one corner out of the way, the remains of tins half-hidden under stones, with their lids turned inwards and, most important of all for John Thornton, his daughter's and Jimmie's handkerchiefs hanging on the ledge where, on that first day, they had put them to dry after cleansing Hunter's wound.

He grabbed them at once, feeling their hardened surface, and somehow knowing they had been stained with blood, and later washed. Duncan Walsh, examining them also, was of the same opinion. 'There's your answer for the children being out every day and taking that meat with them. They've been looking after my Hunter who was injured.' He directed the rays of the torch on to the bed Margaret and Jimmie had made for him, and his keen eyes saw the pellets the girl had succeeded in squeezing from the wounded flank. 'The dog was shot at by someone!' he exclaimed angrily. 'Here are the pellets they got out of the wound!' He indicated them amongst the other debris in the cave. 'Your kids have been great!' he said huskily.

'But where are they now?' John enquired anxiously.

'Obviously cut off by that heath fire,' Duncan answered at once. 'It seems your assumption in that direction was right. I've a feeling they got Hunter's injuries healed up and were bringing him home by a different route. They'll be perfectly safe. Hunter will see to that. Now cease being wae.' This was Duncan's first use of an ancient Scots word, and John did not understand. Seeing the other did not comprehend him, Duncan added hastily, 'I mean don't be unhappy. We know now what's really happened. They were here this morning, and Max will very soon hunt them out. Not for nothing has he won cups for his exceptional tracking abilities. We'll bed down until daybreak and start afresh.' Seeing the consternation on John's face and feeling he was about to object, the other said kindly: 'Think about it. It's best. We'll feel more able to face a new day after a rest; anyway, at the end of it all, Max will probably lead us back to Rosgill where you'll find all three, the children trying to explain ... and possibly failing.'

'I'll understand all right,' John replied, agreeing to Duncan's suggestion.

'Aye, you would because you've seen for yourself what happened. Now for that nap.'

He lay on the bed the children had originally made for Hunter, rolling over on to his side so that Max could occupy part of it also. Soon he was asleep, but John Thornton crouched, unsleeping, against the wall, his head resting on the rucksack, his eyes staring out of the cleft waiting for the first hint of daylight as had done Duncan Walsh's favourite dog, Hunter, before him.

As with Margaret and Jimmie in their hidden valley, he found the new day a long time dawning; but at last the darkness thinned into a scarcely discernible greyness, then slowly the nearest objects took on tangible shapes outside the cave, then he could see the track leading down the fell to Gatescarth Pass, and a few scattered boulders.

'Duncan,' whispered John, to the man still sleeping on what must have been a very uncomfortable bed of moss and reeds. He put out a hand to shake him awake, but a warning growl from Max warned him that he alone had the right. He did so vigorously, pushing his nose into his master's back.

'Hullo, Max,' he remarked, struggling to awake and at the same time to remember exactly where he was. Then seeing John Thornton looking down at him he recalled all too clearly why he was sleeping rough and the discoveries they had made on arrival at this place of rocks . . . 'Hunter's cave', he named it now, not Harter Fell.

'Breakfast?' queried John, pulling another package of sandwiches from his coat pocket. 'I thought we might need some more, and got Ellen to make them up while you were having your supper.'

Duncan grinned amiably. 'Thank goodness for that,' he said. 'It'll take the edge off any hunger we might feel.

There's some coffee left too. . . .' He held up the flask and shook it. 'After a bite and what remains of the coffee, we'll away. Max will make no mistakes. You can bank on that, and it may well turn out as I said before we went asleep.'

John refrained from telling his companion that he had slept but little, but nodded agreeably, conscious that there was little else he *could* do since everything certainly now rested with the tracking qualities of the alsatian.

Both men washed and refreshed themselves as best they could at the beck, near the very spot where Hunter had killed the hare while the collie looked on, and where at other times the dog often lapped water after his morning meal with Margaret and Jimmie.

In the meantime, Max, freed of the long leash, was casting around the foot of the rocks. He had picked up Hunter's scent by the bank, and nosing his way back to the outcrop, was endeavouring to appraise the varying scents left by the children. Here, those of Margaret, Jimmie and Hunter were confused by the intrusion of yet another. It was more recent and was a smell that irritated him. His instincts, going back a long way to those who, in the dim past, had been his ancestors, told him that it was evil, and the hackles on his back stiffened. The two men by this time had returned, ready to resume the search.

Watching Max through experienced eyes, Duncan murmured: 'Somebody else has been here since the children left with Hunter. Whoever it was seems an objectionable type of fellow, judging from Max's reactions.'

'A poacher, most likely,' was John's comment.

'Could be, I suppose.'

'Or somebody after your reward money,' John Thornton replied, unable to keep the note of anxiety out of his voice.

'That, of course, is a distinct possibility,' Duncan answered thoughtfully.

'Now, let's get down to finding your children and Hunter,' he said abruptly, turning to John with a confident smile. 'I expect they're home by now, but we'll follow the trail they took.' Then to Max he said, 'Heel!' The dog came at once to his master's bidding, and the long leash was again attached to the dog's collar. Pulling Jimmie's shirt from his pocket, he uttered the word to which John Thornton was now accustomed. Max sniffed the article, sniffed also diligently around the entrance to the cave, and finally being satisfied that he had picked up the scent of the boy intermingled with that of the girl and Hunter, ignored that other repulsive smell, and strode rapidly forward to the distant grassy height of Branstree. His movement quickened, but was evenly paced to enable his master and the man with him to keep up. The alien scent was still the strongest, but he was not deterred. He knew the one, indeed the three he was to follow, and in the daylight his progress was easier, for he could see the obstacles in his way.

'They made off for Branstree after leaving Harter,' said John, pointing to a small cairn at the summit of a long, grassy, flat-topped hill. 'It's going to be a long climb to the pass if that's the way they went.'

'Could they get to Rosgill that way?' Duncan asked.

'They could if they took the lower slope to Gatescarth, which we know they didn't. Max there followed a straight scent last night, direct to Harter Fell.'

Duncan nodded, not answering, wondering how this fresh, new day would finally end. He had not the slightest doubt that Max would supply the answer.

Max did indeed find the answer, a little sooner than was expected. John had told his new friend that it was his firm belief that the children with Hunter had hoped to reach Rosgill by way of Shap Fells, and had been driven back by the heath fire. Little knowing how right he was in this assumption, he then guessed that finding it dark and much too late to cross the fells, and possibly frightened by the spread of the fire, they had returned to the valley behind Branstree, and stayed the night in some protected hollow. He described the strath to Duncan, saying: 'It is so seldom visited, hardly coming within the actual confines of Lakeland as so described by the guide books. Yet, it is very beautiful. . . .'

It was as he said this that they reached the smooth ascent to the pass. Max's pace had visibly slackened; there were more confusing scents here, the three he was most interested in seeming very fresh, an hour or so old at the most, the fainter scents going upwards to the pass at the summit of the long sprawl of green-backed mountain.

The dog was very hesitant. He sniffed the ground constantly as if a trifle perplexed. Duncan Walsh watched him intently, waiting for the animal's next decisive move. After a second or two, Max moved slowly up the slope, halting, after a few yards, before a ledge of protruding rock upon which a wet stain showed quite clearly. He sniffed this eagerly, his ears erect and his tail plumed, rising to the level of his back. Then to both Duncan's and John's surprise he swung about, lifting his leg and leaving his own mark on the ledge.

His master, with his wide knowledge of dogs, understood this action, for Max had discovered Hunter's own recent visit to the spot, and was redirected back to the scents at the foot of Branstree. Once again at the place where the confused trails were intermingled his nose went once more to the ground to establish the direction he should take. All that his master had taught him in training, all the instinctive knowledge of those who had never been sheep-herding dogs, but animals rigidly trained in the tracking down of fugitives from the law, was awakened in him now to a higher degree. Confident and eager, he set off at a swift loping stride along the foot of the hill.

'What do you make of that?' John Thornton asked in astonishment.

Duncan looked at him speculatively, wondering if his companion was losing faith in his dog's capabilities. So sure was he of his knowledge of the dogs he bred, he answered a little drily: 'The children and Hunter undoubtedly did as you yourself said . . . spent the night in that strath you mentioned, and at daybreak set off for home. That stain on the rock was where Hunter lifted his leg to relieve himself. Max found it and did the same. Och! Don't be fretting yourself, man. That was the clue that cleared up the doubt of a muddled trail. We're well set on the last stages of the hunt now, laddie. . . .'

He was unquestionably right. Max was losing no time; the scents were strong in his nostrils now and he was urged to strain at the leash and break into the characteristic lope of a police dog near its objective.

Ahead of him, where the slope they followed faltered and became moorland comprised of tussock-grass and heather, was a beck, and beyond it the gaping entrance of Gatescarth Pass. The dog knew it to be the same place through which he had come in the darkness of the previous night. He pushed on unerringly, reached the beck, and after sniffing boisterously at the bank, waded across, dragging his master with him.

Fortunately for all three, the water of the stream was low, and at this point flowing over a causeway of gravel, held in place by a shelving ledge of rock. The men got across suffering little more than wet feet and dripping trouser bottoms. The head of the pass, hidden between curving daleland ridges, was quite near. As the men waited, watching Max industriously quartering the new ground across the beck, they heard from across the dales the recurring note of the cuckoo, as had been the case of Margaret and Jimmie on many another occasion when they were looking after Hunter.

Suddenly the moment of suspense was over. Max had found the scent again, less strong because of the water the children and the dog had waded across.

He tugged at the leash, straining to be away, pulling his master with him. All three moved quickly along the tussocky moorland, stumbling in the direction of the ridges concealing Gatescarth Pass. The dog's excitement was being communicated to Duncan and John. Both felt that something of momentous importance had been sensed by the straining alsatian. His head was no longer lowered, his muzzle following a trail. Instead it was raised high, the ears pricked, and the nostrils widely flared as he tested out the scents in the breeze. Then the leash went slack as he stopped, and he stood motionless, in the stance associated with his breed.

'He's on to something,' Duncan said tensely.

'I only hope the children have come to no harm,' answered the faltering voice of John Thornton.

Duncan Walsh shook his head. 'Not with Hunter to protect them,' he said.

There was so great a degree of confidence in his voice that Thornton was conscious of immediate relief. He felt he spoke out of a wide and well-founded experience of the dogs he bred, and judging from the marvellous performance put up by Max in his tracking abilities, felt that Margaret and Jimmie would indeed be well protected by Hunter. His mind then seized on another line of thinking, formulated during the anxiety of the last few hours. The children must *really* have a dog of their own, he thought rather belatedly. It's the best I can do for them as they wander about so much in this desolate fell country....

His ruminations and anxieties were rudely interrupted, for from the pass itself came the sound of deep barking – barking that expressed great anger, each individual sound echoing from dale to fell and back again.

'That's Hunter's bark!' Duncan exclaimed in alarm. 'Quick! Something is happening in the pass.'

John Thornton's skin was tightly drawn across his cheeks. 'You don't think . . .?' he began.

'No!' This rather curtly uttered by Duncan Walsh who had so accurately interpreted Thornton's fears. 'There's more to it than you're allowing yourself to suppose. I'll let Max loose.'

Before John could protest, Max, who had recognized Hunter's barking, was away across the moor and into the opposing jaws of the pass, the two men following as quickly as they could, one with a great fear in his heart, the other with alarm, but tempered with relief at having at last found his dog.

'He's putting up a fight for those kids, but against whom?' he muttered as he ran. 'Against whom?'

*   *   *

Up to that point, Jimmie and Margaret had negotiated without mishap their way home until they turned into the seclusion of Gatescarth Pass. Margaret, weary though she was, had begun to sing while Jimmie started to whistle. Neither had noticed that Hunter was suspiciously testing out the air-streams, the hackles on his back slowly rising. Then at a spot where the pass, enclosed within high ridges, made a sharp turn eastward to the approaches of Mardale Common, the alsatian's suspicions were more than just confirmed. To the children's horror and surprise, they encountered the gipsy, crouched behind a deeply embedded slab of rock, grinning with sadistic delight. The tune Margaret had been singing changed to a cry of alarm, and Jimmie's whistling to a cry of defiance as he stood in front of his sister with clenched fists and legs set widely apart to offset any assault that might be made on him.

The gipsy also had been taken somewhat by surprise, but Jimmie's whistling had given him ample warning. He had been making his way back to the camp, thinking the Thornton kids had somehow, by stealth and cunning, evaded him. Now, at sight of them with the dog worth fifty pounds, all the viciousness in his nature came to the surface – worse even than when he had fired the gorse.

Already the net was off his shoulder, and he was holding it stretched to its widest limits in order to snare the dog. He was sure it was all going to be so easy. He had expected the children to flee on seeing him, and was disconcerted when Jimmie stood his ground, his sister close behind. He made his greatest mistake as regards Hunter. The dog was no fool. Knowing it was his duty to protect the children, he crouched low, his hind legs firmly placed for the leap he intended making. He was growling savagely and showing his teeth.

The leap when he made it had all the force of his weight behind it. He went straight for the net in the gipsy's outstretched arms, the force and ferocity of the attack throwing the man backwards so that it was he who became enmeshed in the net and not Hunter!

One lasting impression he retained in the depths of his

twisted mind as he hurtled backwards was the upward thrust of the powerful grey shape of the alsatian, a snarl wrinkling its muzzle, all the pent-up fury in him suggesting that he was intent on mauling his victim to death. Just one half-articulate cry the gipsy uttered, a cry frantic and hysterical. In an impulsive move to protect himself, he rolled away from the dog, becoming more caught up in

the net until he was utterly entangled in it, as had been the salmon he had so gleefully watched on the Solway Firth. For them it had been death. For him, what? Hunter, however, did not press further the assault he had made. He had achieved his purpose by making the gipsy completely powerless to commit further trouble. He had actually jumped back as the gipsy fell, threshing about with arms and legs. Knowing the man could no longer harm the children, the dog stood over the prostrate form, his tongue quivering between panting jaws, but still with a dangerous, threatening light in his eyes. He then gave the gipsy further warning, for he barked and barked, each note a paean of satisfaction that echoed far and wide.

By now, Max came racing into the pass, and went immediately to what he considered was Hunter's assistance. Taking his cue from the other, he stood snarling over the thoroughly demoralized gipsy, who screamed with terror, quite unable to contain himself any longer. Whilst an agonizing sense of horror struck deeply into him, making him shut his eyes, he yet had sufficient sense to keep completely still, and his screaming ended in a smothered gurgling as he became semi-conscious.

It was at this stage that John Thornton and Duncan Walsh put in a breathless appearance.

'Father!' cried Margaret, rushing into her parent's outstretched arms just as Hunter, leaving his kennel companion to keep guard over the gipsy, leapt whining and crying joyfully to Duncan. As he reared up, placing his paws on his master's shoulders, the man's grasp around his huge frame was firm and yet strangely gentle, and in an instant that old affinity of complete reunification made them seem as one. . . .

Jimmie also had joined his father, stammering in an effort to explain. 'Don't bother. We know!' Out of the corner of his eye he noticed Duncan's slender fingers moving slowly across Hunter's smooth skull, while the man was murmuring words his ears could not hear. Notwithstanding, the dog understood their meaning, for his tail waved furiously, and his tongue tentatively flicked his master's cheek in an act of devotion.

Thornton, to relieve the tension of reunion, asked his son if he had some cord with which to effectively secure the gipsy. Jimmie produced from his copious pocket the length of cord he had used earlier as a leash for Hunter.

Five minutes later, with the children and dogs looking on, John and Duncan had tied the gipsy up in the net, leaving only his legs free. Then hauling him none too gently to his feet they led the man through the pass to Rosgill *en route* for Bampton and the police, with Max and Hunter on either side of him.

At Rosgill John Thornton sent the children hurrying up to the house where their mother and Aunt Ellen were waiting in the living room, both suffering from nervous tension. 'Tell your mother we'll be home in a short while, after we have left this chap with the police,' he shouted after them.

Duncan followed the children, remarking he was getting his car. 'Max will keep guard over the gipsy fellow. ... You'd better stay with him!'

As he ran up the drive and past the summer house amidst the rhododendrons, John could not fail to notice that Hunter loped close beside him. Obviously, the dog had no intention of ever letting his master out of his sight again. He fell to wondering what both man and dog had endured mentally over the separation, and then regarded thoughtfully Max, who stood with his muzzle within an inch or two of the gipsy's leg. John eyed the animal with undisguised appraisal and respect, muttering, 'He knows exactly what he has to do.'

He turned his head as Duncan drove his estate car into the road with Hunter seated upright in the rear seat.

Not a minute was lost as the gipsy was bundled into the back, white-faced and shaking, with Max leaping in beside him. John took his place beside Duncan, saying, 'Those dogs of yours put up a marvellous show.'

'They always do,' was the brief reply.

Not long afterwards, they were on the return journey, the gipsy handcuffed and locked up in the one stout place in the cottage outhouse that could be called a cell.

There was the scent of wild thyme and heather in the air, with just a trace of burning from off Shap, but it was a wonderful morning as the men drove on to Rosgill, with two happy dogs seated behind them.

They turned into the drive of the house to be greeted by another, entirely different smell – that of breakfast being prepared. Both the men and dogs realized just how hungry they were. All explanations would have to wait until after they had eaten.

Supper at Roskill that evening was a great success. All strain had gone, and Hunter, now reunited with his beloved master, never left his side, while Max, having taken a very special liking to Jimmie and Margaret, remained close to them. John Thornton was so grateful for Duncan's help in finding the children that over the meal he suggested that perhaps Walsh might like to stay on at Rosgill for a week or so. Duncan, who certainly wanted to make a few more sketches of the district, and complete a painting he had started earlier before the Hunter incident, hesitated before replying, saying eventually that the Thorntons might find it trying with two large dogs about the place.

To the surprise of everybody, it was Aunt Ellen who protested, remarking that the dogs could do no harm, and Mary Thornton agreed wholeheartedly. Duncan found himself persuaded, and rang his hotel in Patterdale saying he would be collecting his baggage and leaving in the morning.

That night, while the gipsy, and also his wife who had been taken into custody, dozed fitfully, captive in the dark outhouse of the so-called police station, Duncan slept in the guest room with Hunter beside his bed, curled snugly on his own blanket brought from the car. Max was comfortable on a similar rug in the summer house and all explanations satisfactorily disposed of, Margaret and Jimmie, fully relieved of their varied anxieties, slept soundly until another morning broke in brightening colour over the hills.

Whilst the children slept a little longer than usual and

the sun was well up by the time they got down to breakfast, they appeared greatly refreshed, and after an appetizing meal specially prepared for them, asked if they could go for a walk on the fells until luncheon.

'It will be a little later today,' their mother told them. 'Aunt Ellen is being driven into Penrith to catch a train for the north, and Mr Walsh is going to Patterdale to collect his things from the hotel.' As the children looked at Hunter, who had greeted them with enthusiasm and affection, they saw at once that he was not going to let his master out of his sight.

Duncan himself proposed they took Max with them. 'He'd love a long run, and you'll find he's exceedingly obedient, and absolutely reliable with sheep, so you'll have no fears on that account.'

The children's joyful reaction made their father think once again that he must surely get them a dog of their own. . . . A border collie, he thought.

Max, already in the house after a long rest in the summer house, knew he had been the subject of discussion, and when Jimmie and Margaret prepared to go out, and his master handed them a leash which he recognized as his own, he knew he was to accompany them. Quivering and whining with excitement, while the now more solemn-minded Hunter looked on, he was at the door first when the children set off.

Max went bounding on ahead, looking back occasionally with what Margaret called 'happy laughing eyes' to ensure they were following. When they came to the head of Hawes Water and the dog continued on following the track to the pass, it was the girl who called him back, saying, 'This way, Max.' As they swung westward down the narrow valley and the lake, Margaret noticed her brother's silence, indulging, she decided, 'in one of his queer moods'. In this she was not far wrong.

That day with Hunter had been such a memorable

day, and they had been so happy, that he was doubting it could ever be repeated. Days like that came but once; what followed was but the shadow of a memory. Yet, was it? The lake when they came to it was as blue as before, splintered here and there where sunlight was reflected from rippling waves. The scents were the same, but while the cuckoo's call was absent, the mewling cry of the buzzard seemed a never-ceasing thing.

The children sat where they had rested previously, while Max, picking up Hunter's scent, quested to and fro sniffing contentedly, pausing now and again to look at Jimmie and Margaret with happy, joyous eyes.

After a while he joined them, thrusting himself between them, thrilling to the touch of the girl's hand on his head and back. 'He's very beautiful,' Margaret said. 'He's so different in colouring from Hunter.'

'He's what I heard Mr Walsh call "black and tan", while he said Hunter was "dark sable",' Jimmie answered.

Impulsively, Margaret put both arms around the dog, as she had often done with Hunter, her fingers probing deeply into the gold ruffle about his neck. The fur, she thought, was the softest she had ever felt.

'He's lovely,' she breathed quietly, but Jimmie, hearing her words, said sharply, 'Don't get the same ideas about him as we did over Hunter. Max is Mr Walsh's dog, highly trained, and will go back to Langholm with him. I've no doubt we shall be able to persuade Father to get us a dog now, but it will only be a border collie . . . not an alsatian.'

Margaret nodded her head slowly, her fingers still probing deeply into Max's fur, but thinking that there was something different about an alsatian. They seemed to understand so much and were lovely to look at.

Jimmie was far from feeling his usual self, more moody than he had ever known before. His introspective thinking had become deeper than he really knew, and in response to that call, and the movement and sound of the lake on the shore, he told himself that it was just a case of remembering one wonderful day when they were here, and thought it the best day of their lives. . . .

'Come, Maggie!' he said sharply, scrambling to his feet as if to escape from himself and his thoughts, shattering his sister's dream.

Somehow, that abrupt action had brought him out of his reminiscence of things past and done, and by the time they were well set on the road to Rosgill, Jimmie had regained his good spirits and was throwing an odd stick or two for Max to retrieve.

Although they were in good time for luncheon, John Thornton and Duncan Walsh were back from their respective journeys, standing at the windows of the sitting room looking out over the fells. John was speculatively tapping a large envelope in the palm of his left hand with marked reluctance at having taken it.

'Here they come,' Duncan said quietly, breaking the silence between them, 'and Max looking as if he had never enjoyed himself so much before.'

John admitted this to be the case, adding: 'The children look very happy also.'

'They should have a dog of their own,' his friend said. 'They'd look after him very well indeed. Look what they did for Hunter. . . .' He again remarked on what the veterinary surgeon in Patterdale told him. 'Not only did they get all the pellets out of his flank, they bathed the wounds with soothing oil and antiseptic, thus saving the dog greater discomfort and undoubtedly aiding the healing process. They also combed him pretty thoroughly, keeping him free of sheep ticks and his coat glossy and unmatted. . . .'

John nodded thoughtfully. 'They can use their brains when called upon to do so.'

'So, you see, they really should have a dog to look after.'

'I'm thinking very seriously about it.'

Duncan Walsh was about to say something further when the children and Max burst into the room, stopping all further conversation, Max and Hunter sniffing noses and waving their tails in greeting, and the children looking at their parent enquiringly. John and Duncan merely enquired if they had enjoyed their morning with Max.

They replied vigorously that they had, Margaret having forgotten entirely her brother's moroseness.

The men exchanged sudden glances of approval, smiling as if everything was turning out as they had expected.

Jimmie and Margaret were surprised when their father announced that on coming back from Penrith he had called in at their school and had obtained an extension of their holiday for a further week. He said there had been no difficulty over the matter, since everybody in Bampton, and even people in Penrith itself, had heard of their devotion to the injured Hunter and the grave danger they had encountered from the gipsy. Then, without prior warning, between courses, he produced the envelope he had been carrying in his inside pocket, merely saying that it was for them. 'Mr Walsh insists on you having the fifty pounds' reward money, although I was dubious about it.'

They took the envelope quietly, both thanking Duncan Walsh and agreeing with their father that they really didn't deserve it, but just did what they felt had to be done for Hunter.

'You did more than that,' Duncan answered gravely. 'Those long walks up to the fell, and the care you took of him, deserves more than money.' There was an underlying significance in his tones as he spoke which their father could not fail to notice.

Later that afternoon, after Margaret and Jimmie had assisted in clearing up in the kitchen, the two men and children, accompanied by the dogs, took a stroll over to the Abbey – the objective Jimmie, Margaret and Hunter had failed to reach.

'I must get down to some serious painting and sketching while I'm here,' Duncan was heard to remark. 'This time I'll not let my work deter me from keeping an eye on Hunter. I couldn't go through all that suspense and torment again.'

John Thornton, ever a practical man in all things with strong family ties, and not given to what he considered undue sentimentalism, just gave the other a quick glance, but made no answer. He nevertheless thought all the more, happy indeed that it *was* his children who had brought Duncan's much-loved dog back to him. He was very proud of them, not only for that, but for the danger and hardships they had endured in doing so. It then came to him that there was a deal more common sense and determination in them than he had hitherto suspected. Even they had fallen under the spell of Hunter, and he shook his head, wondering. . . .

'Dogs,' he muttered under his breath. 'What is it they have that makes for so much happiness and pain?'

Hunter was close at his master's heels, but Max was running on ahead with Jimmie and Margaret, barking with utter abandonment and joy when one or the other of them threw a stick for him to retrieve. He decided there and then that he would set about finding them a suitable animal . . . a puppy, perhaps, who would grow up with them. Involuntarily he looked down again at Hunter, who was more concerned with being with his master than chasing along with his kennel companion. He thought he was beginning to understand Duncan's attitude towards his own special dog, even his great affection for him, a little better. Hunter had been brought up as a young dog by Duncan and there was a deep bond between them as a result. The words 'one-man dogs' flittered across his mind, and he thought that was the real answer.

They returned home to Rosgill as the sun which had been shimmering with springtime heat all day was now growing deeper and deeper in a tone of paling orange. It appeared to be sinking slowly, making long strands of fleecy cloud, first glowing pink with colour, then dark along the eastern flanks of the Cumbrian Mountains. Fell birds went wheeling by overhead to their nesting sites in the hidden valleys known only by them. Along the last mile home, a faint mist started to rise as the dew fell, and evening walked that last long mile with them.

The first star was out as they turned up the drive, and the after-glow was fast dying behind the summits of the distant mountains of the west. Only the lakes in the hollows of the hills seemed to hold some resemblance of what had been the day, and later they too would be dark, with the stars and perhaps a crescent moon shining in them.

Lamp-glow showed behind the drawn curtains of the house at Rosgill where two men and a woman sat talking before a log fire.

There were many such nights for Duncan Walsh to enjoy before he returned north to Langholm, and a firm relationship grew up between himself and his hosts. He and Hunter set out each morning, sometimes for the day, always accompanied by a pad for sketching, canvases and easel. There was, he explained, as he put a very expensive camera in the car, so much he wanted to do in Lakeland.

John and his wife Mary noticed that he never encouraged Max to go with him on his working journeys. He even went so far as to say on one occasion that the dog was much happier with the children, which, on consideration by their parents, seemed to be the case.

These days in early spring, with the heather glowing purple on the fells and daffodils giving a blink of yellow in the most unexpected places, were days the Thorntons were to remember with pleasure long after Duncan Walsh had gone his way home across the border. Jimmie and Margaret had seemed happier than they had been for a long time, finding a fitting companionship with the dog.

Their father had already promised them an animal of their own, something he knew they had always desired. Meanwhile everywhere they went Max, Duncan's alsatian, went with them, learning quickly every aspect of the fells and dales, every footpath, and enjoying his brief swims in the small tarns alongside which the children rested and ate their lunch, giving him his share as so recently they had done with Hunter.

It was as though they still had Hunter with them, a happier Hunter, it was true. His difference in colouring made not the slightest impression on their minds, for his general traits were those of Hunter and all his breed. They got the utmost pleasure in secretly dropping a handkerchief, or something similar, and getting him to track back and find it which he always did with obvious enjoyment, sitting before them on his return as taught by his master.

'I wonder if Mr Walsh would accept that fifty pounds for him?' Margaret suggested one day.

Jimmie's head-shaking was angry and emphatic. 'It would be an insult after he has given us the money. Besides, Max must be worth almost as much to him as Hunter.'

Despite her bitter disappointment and her acknowledgement that her brother was right as usual, she still permitted herself to dwell on the matter, regarding it as a worth-while dream for the present, and even for the future, giving them memories to cling to when they no longer had the dog.

They discussed the matter no further, continuing to gaze with admiration at Max, who was loping along a lakeside in an easy, questing manner. He reminded them so much of Hunter whom they had come to love, little realizing that they were allowing themselves to feel the same way about Max.

There seemed another heart-break coming to them.

The Thornton children had a special name for this unexpected extension of their holiday from school because of the many long rambles they took over the fells with Max. Hunter they could not fail to notice always greeted them with enthusiasm and affection when they came down in the morning, and afterwards became once more the inseparable companion of his master, accompanying him everywhere on his painting and sketching expeditions. It seemed to the children he was afraid to let Duncan out of his sight, and somehow, in a way that hurt them, they came to the dim understanding of the suffering the dog had endured at loss of his master.

Because of this, they often wondered at the exuberance Max displayed when out with them. It was as though he preferred the new life he was experiencing instead of that at Langholm. He seemed to be concentrating all his attention and affection on them, hence the name Margaret and Jimmie gave to this additional holiday – 'the golden days of spring'; and golden they truly were, for the sun shone constantly in an almost cloudless sky, and what rain did fall was either during the night or very early morning.

As if by common consent between the two, neither Jimmie nor Margaret permitted themselves to think too deeply on their growing relationship with Max, or to give voice to the tangible knowledge that the 'golden days' must certainly come to an end before the week was out when Duncan Walsh and the dogs were to return to Dumfries-shire. They had heard him say that the Thornton family must visit him in the summer, and with this they both had to be content.

Perhaps consolation might be had from the fact that they were to have a dog of their own, but that, they knew in their hearts, would not compensate them for the loss of both Hunter and Max... certainly not Max, Margaret often thought despondently, remembering how, in almost every detail except colouring, he resembled Hunter. He possessed also the same endearing qualities and deep capacity for showing his affection for them.

On the Thursday – for them possibly the last day with Max – they planned a day's outing. They discussed the idea with their father, all three peering over a large-scale map of the district. 'We'd like to make a nice long day of it,' his daughter whispered. 'As Mr Walsh is returning to Langholm soon, it will be our last real outing with Max...'

Next morning dawned bright and sunny. It had all the appearances of being the best day yet. Margaret and Jimmie were up early, as were their father and mother. The large rucksack was used for their provisions. 'With your food is the remainder of that carcass for Max,' their father said with a laugh of amusement.

The two, joined by Duncan and Hunter, watched the children striding off in the direction of the head of Hawes Water, Max well in advance with wildly waving tail. His deep barks of excitement echoed back at them, causing Duncan to smile and remark softly, 'It seems to me, they suit each other.'

Husband and wife exchanged glances, but made no comment. Their children were very dear to them, and above all else they desired their complete happiness.

This was the route the children had at first taken to reach Hunter in his refuge on Harter Fell. Their hearts, however, were not too downcast. Max himself was far too excitable for that, and the day itself so perfect. The air also, that morning, was so clean and translucent that by the time they had rounded the tip of the lake and climbed the southern shoulder of High Street, Ullswater, the white houses of Patterdale, and the rolling fells towards Grisdale with its small tarn below Helvellyn, were crystal clear.

The tarn itself shone out like the lightly held piece of the sky itself, and it had all the appearance of being so purely evanescent that it must vanish with the next intake of breath. Only the ridge of Helvellyn had real substance, reaching up and ever upwards above that silver blink of light which Margaret said would be their objective.

'It's a long way off yet,' Jimmie answered, shading his eyes the better to evaluate the distance.

'We've a good pair of legs on us,' his sister replied authoritatively.

'We certainly have,' was Jimmie's brief comment, and shouting to Max, went scrambling rapidly down High Street in the direction of Angle Tarn and Breda Fell. In spite of the children's burst of activity, Max was quicker than either, leaping ahead of them with joy, halting only when called.

They undoubtedly made excellent progress, and after crossing the main road to Patterdale finally came out of the valley from Bridgend to make a more restrained assault on the steeply rising fells to Grisdale Pass. Now and again they had brief glimpses of Helvellyn and its scree slopes of Striding Ridge.

With a good half-hour to go before midday, they reached the tarn with its undiminished brightness, and flinging down the rucksack, took their ease amongst the tussocky grass with Max lying panting beside them.

They ate their lunch, and lay back, partially shaded by the tall reeds surrounding them. Max, with his back as a pillow for their heads, breathed gently, satisfied with his own share of the meat they had brought, and blissfully happy in the knowledge that they were all together. Drowsy, like the children, he permitted himself a doze, the breeze, fey and wandering like a lost thing over the tarn, keeping away the heat of midday that was intense because of the cloudless sky. No bird called here, but a thousand unheard sounds struggled to give utterance deep in the fertile earth, full with the stirring of a new life yet to reach fruition. The scent of heather and young bracken was already a sign of it . . . a scent of summer yet to come. . . . Summer in all its glory of Lakeland splendour. . . .

*   *   *

Back at Rosgill, with tea over, and Mary Thornton taking her afternoon rest, Duncan asked John if he would like to see the work he had done while he had been staying with them. 'There are a couple of good canvases, and they should be dry by now,' he explained. 'One is actually based on the sketch I was engaged on when I lost Hunter.'

John was only too pleased to view Duncan Walsh's work, and went eagerly to the latter's room on the first floor.

The room was exceptionally neat and tidy, with canvases and sketches carefully arranged for packing. The paintings were of lakes and mountains and, as far as John could judge, more than expertly executed. This applied also to the sketches which showed a great degree of craftsmanship.

John refrained from praiseworthy comment, sensing Duncan might feel discomfited. He contented himself by saying that all he had been shown had given him an entirely different outlook on art and the work that went into it.

Duncan nodded, highly satisfied, placing canvases and

sketches together ready for placing in the canvas carrier he had specially made for transporting such bulky items easily.

'About that dog for your children,' he said abruptly. 'When are you going to get him?'

'Tomorrow, perhaps,' John answered promptly. 'You see, I have it in mind to travel as far as Penrith with you. There's a good pet shop in the town.'

Duncan shook his head in disapproval. 'You shouldn't buy a dog like that. In any case, you don't need one. You already have a dog.'

John looked at Duncan incredulously. Duncan returned the look steadily before replying to the unasked question: 'I want you to keep Max as a special present from me to the children.'

Thornton was about to protest, but Duncan checked him by asking: 'Is it a smaller dog you prefer?'

'No, but he's valuable to you.'

'All the more reason the children should have him. They'll look after him all right. That's settled then,' forestalling any further protest from John. 'I'll send you his papers and transfer form as soon as I get home. . . .'

He walked over to the window saying: 'The only pity of it is that when a dog becomes a part of you and your daily way of life, you must weigh up the happiness you get from him against the heart-break that must, in the natural course of things, one day follow. . . .'

John Thornton, never a sentimentalist, felt deeply moved.

Duncan turned suddenly from the window. He said calmly: 'I'm glad we've settled Max's future. He'll be happier as a family dog than just one amongst others in a kennel. . . .'

Mary Thornton was delighted when she heard the news, and said they must start making Max feel that this was his home that very night. 'He must become part of the family at once,' was her final remark.

The sunset that night was of rare beauty as it flamed over the Cumbrian Mountains. Colour filled every valley of the west, and Duncan, watching it from one window with Mary and John at another, thought he had never seen anything quite like it save in the Hebrides. The windows were slightly opened and the scents of bushes and flowers came in on a warm breeze. 'I can see the children and Max coming down the track beside the beck,' Duncan heard Mary say to her husband. A blackbird was singing, his last song for the evening.

Then the voices of Margaret and Jimmie came to him, the voices of youth; and as the blackbird flew off with a warning note to its mate, he saw them coming up the drive with Max walking between them, each holding his collar, the dog looking from one to the other with waving tail.

'He'll be very happy indeed with them,' Duncan muttered.

Mary Thornton hastened to the door to let them in and he heard their joyful exclamations as she told them the news about Max.

Duncan drew in his breath with joy at the children's cry of happiness.

'Bring him right in,' Duncan heard Mary Thornton say as his fingers rested gently on Hunter's head. 'No more summer house for Max . . . he's one of us now.'

Margaret and Jimmie came running into the room to thank him, and for an instant he ceased petting Hunter to put his arms around them both as they continued to utter their thanks. 'He'll be a great companion to you,' was all he could say, giving them a brief hug. Duncan heard Margaret say how grateful they both were for his kindness. He just smiled in reply.

While their voices were still expressing their great joy,

a cold nose touched the back of his hand, and again his slender fingers moved lovingly over the head of the dog who claimed his heart.

Planned at
Patterdale,
Ullswater,
in the Lake District
of England.

Completed at
Araglin, in the
Knockmealdown Mountains
of Co. Waterford,
Ireland.

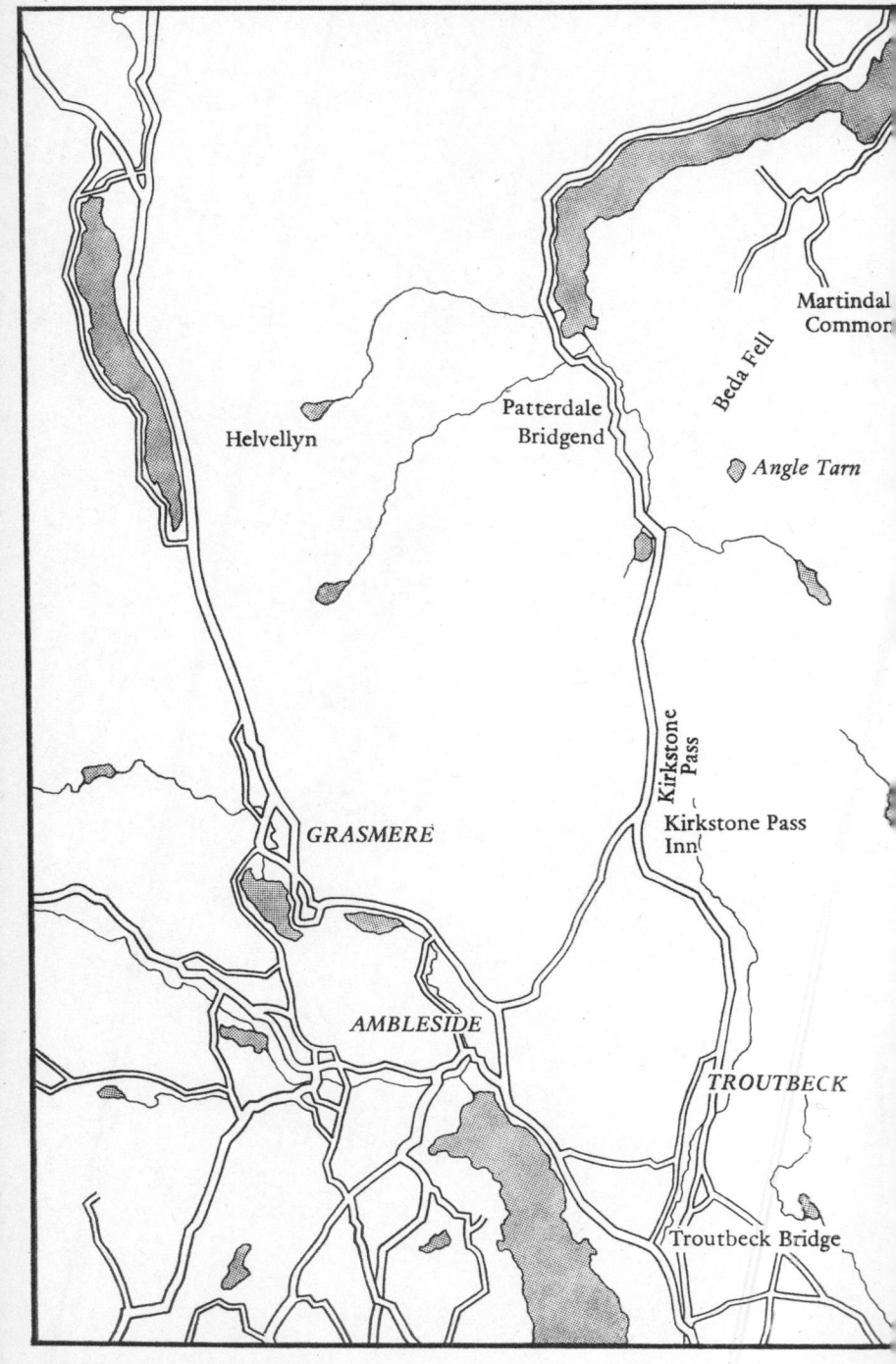